Spanish Harlem

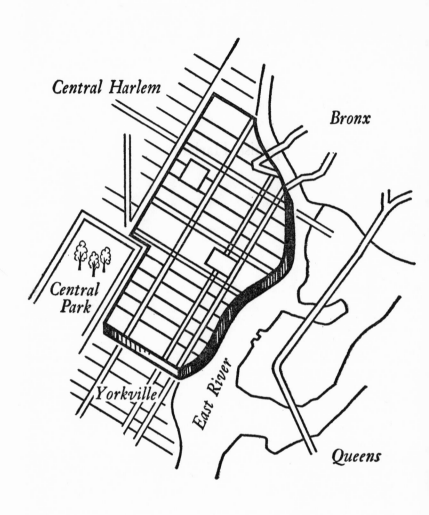

Central Harlem

Bronx

Central
Park

Yorkville

East River

Queens

AN ANATOMY OF POVERTY

PATRICIA CAYO SEXTON

SPANISH HARLEM

HARPER & ROW, Publishers
New York · Evanston · London

M-R

LIBRARY OF CONGRESS CATALOG CARD NUMBER: 65-11717

66318

To my mother
ALICE CAYO LINDSEY
a generous woman who has known hard times and who,
along with the residents of East Harlem,
deserves much more than this

Contents

vii

Preface

In Spanish Harlem the anatomy of city poverty is revealed: slum housing, congestion, illiteracy, the overwhelming adjustment of the rural migrant to big-city life, and an unusual intensity of being. Less visible are the good omens and rays of light, but they are there.

The city's face and its future, with some of its scars enlarged, are there in Spanish Harlem. The community is one of a family of faces: New York, the United States, every city, and every nation. The riddles in its slums and aspiring people are continuous with those hidden in the larger society.

All the big issues are there, along with the poor, the jobless, the dropouts, the violent, the desperate, and tens of thousands of normal people. I was scheduled to spend two weeks in Spanish (or East*) Harlem, but I spent almost two years, held by a drama more compelling than anything I have seen on stage in many years. The struggle is a real one. It is a struggle to be alive and healthy.

* The Negro sections of the Northern district are not, strictly speaking, part of Spanish Harlem, a term applied more to the southern Puerto Rican areas; but they are tied by poverty and proximity to what has come to be known as East Harlem.

Given the prevailing folklore about crime in the slums, the stranger approaches with caution. Once inside, he finds it difficult to break loose. The population is diverse and engaging. The street life is more vivid than improvised theater. There is passion and conflict.

For the student of society, there are also the intriguing mysteries of the social organism, waiting like a buried city to be explored. The individual is particular and personal and his story, well told, is usually of interest to the listener. But the social order creates the individual and his story. It is author and creator, and its mysteries are even more fascinating to explore.

The questions to be asked are endless. The sociologist asks most. He looks for clues to help answer the questions: Where are we now? Where do we go from here if present trends continue? And the most dangerous question of all: Where *should* we go from here, given what we know of the social order and of human aspirations?

This book has two major purposes. It undertakes to draw a rather detailed portrait of East Harlem so that the reader can see more clearly what a "slum" looks like. And it also seeks to identify problems and solutions in the slum. Often only the questions will be formulated, a large job in itself. In some cases the answers of others will be given, and in some cases my own. Social change— what to do and how to do it—will be a theme in all the questions and answers.

I have tried to restrain a natural urge to preach. And since these waters are so unchartered, I have sought to avoid drawing glib conclusions from mixed and uncompleted evidence. I do not believe there is an "Only Way" to upgrade slums. There are many ways. The purpose of the volume is both *de*scriptive and *pre*scriptive: to describe some of the patient's behavior, appearance, symptoms, and then to prescribe some possible medications. Preventatives will be preferred to placebos.

Most problems in East Harlem seem to merge into one: How can people best be organized to deal with their own problems and to get enough power to demand of society what is their right—decent jobs at decent wages, decent housing and good schools, and opportunities at least equal to those enjoyed by most other

Americans. Many claim that the poor cannot be organized. Others say it can be done and that it is their only hope. The poor, of course, do not want "to be organized." They want the good things other people have. Organized effort, however, may be the only lasting way to get what they want. It is a means to an end, not an end in itself.

Once it was customary to think of "helping the poor" only through "service" to the individual and the family—the slow nibbling away at problems via casework and individual therapy. Now we have begun to think of groups rather than individuals and wholes rather than parts: rehabilitation of a whole house, a whole block, a whole community. The social action horizons are pushing out. The city itself is one whole. Beyond that are the state and federal boundaries and the nation's economic system, whose health determines the health of the slum. This book considers one boundary, the community, and the resources it has for growth.

I have found that people are rarely pleased with what you write about them and that a single word of criticism mixed with a thousand of praise will offend; and that a single error mixed into a volume of sound fact will be a pretext for dismissal. Though I have only fondness for the people I met in East Harlem (a fact which may try the reader who prefers scandal and criticism), the good intentions of good people can also lead to hell; and, for all the worthy effort, East Harlem is still a slum. But this is much less the fault of those who have tried than of those who have not.

Poverty has entered the public domain. So this book is intended for a general audience of informed citizens who seek some understanding but cannot see the slum because their range is too close or too distant. The topic is a large one, and the treatment is exploratory rather than empirical, putting to use, as perhaps more research should, the scattered data of other available empirical efforts. The project has been a labor of love, unfinanced by research grants, stimulated by my affection for the people of East Harlem, and completed under the warm encouragement and valued advice of my husband, Brendan; Marion K. Sanders, of *Harper's* magazine; and the book's editor, Richard McAdoo, who said all the right things in the right way, a very difficult task.

I am also deeply indebted to Sam Hirsch, Sam and Sherry Kaplan, Preston Wilcox, Bill Kirk, Mildred Zucker, Ellen Lurie, Commissioner Edwin Corsi of East Harlem; to my colleagues Herbert Gans, Erwin Smigel, and Marvin Bressler who read large sections of the manuscript; and to the following who aided in various essential ways: Mary Hofer Farina, David Hobson, Patricia Campo, Patricia Rebecca Sexton, Arthur Floyd, Nora Bowens, George Calvert, Melvin Schoonover, Arthur Grace, Donald Arthur, Ernest Russell, Eva Kerr, Karin Berg, Elizabeth Adler, Katy Taylor. Gratitude is also extended to my associates S. M. Miller and Frank Riessman, who are filled with lively ideas and whose concern for the disadvantaged may offer an object lesson for other scholars.

We are all, of course, indebted to Michael Harrington for having set off this chain reaction, and to the civil rights groups that made the nation examine its conscience and pocketbook.

My obligation to Dr. Kenneth Clark and my admiration are too large to express here: I know of no person who has done more to point us in the right directions.

A lifetime of gratitude goes to Jack and LuVerne Conway whose enduring friendship and aid mean more than I will get around to telling them. Acknowledgment of personal and professional debt is also in order for my associates at New York University: Dan Dodson, Jack Robertson, and the capable deans of the school of education, Daniel Griffiths, and John Payne—and again to Marvin Bressler who is always missed. I extend further thanks to the people of East Harlem and Puerto Rico who offered abundant hospitality.

I am grateful that this exploration led me to the work of two exceptional men—Saul Alinsky, of the Industrial Areas Foundation, and Mitchell Sviridoff, of New Haven's Community Progress—two who seem to agree on nothing except the need for vastly extended social justice. Beyond that I am indebted to Norman Thomas who first put me on this track as a student, and to the labor movement, particularly the United Auto Workers union, which helped keep me on it. Through them I feel part of a vital and resurgent tradition in American life. None of these people or groups can be blamed for any error of fact or view that may be contained herein.

Though I have put these words on paper, the effort that stands behind the print has been largely a joint one with my husband, Brendan Sexton, whose wisdom and unfailing good judgment I have consulted about everything. As education and organization director of the United Auto Workers union, he has quietly pioneered many of the ideas and projects that are now gaining currency in the development of impoverished communities, the inspiration for which grew out of a sense of kinship with the disadvantaged, belief in their potential, and anger at the condition of their lives. It is said that no man is a hero to his wife, but here I must plead an exception.

New York City   P.C.S.
November 1964

Spanish Harlem

With all my love for Princeton I sometimes think my education really began . . . here in this district. It is a sort of school which sets hard lessons and asks difficult questions. What is our democracy worth? . . . Are we preparing well for national safety when so many of our workers cannot even under favorable conditions make the proper living wage?

–NORMAN THOMAS
*on his seven years as minister of an
East Harlem Protestant Church*

1

Heartbreak is only trouble. An unhappy love affair, the death of a parent or a child, are only troubles. If you are in reasonably good health, have a room and adequate food, tobacco and the price of a drink, death and love can be mourned in comfort.
—BRENDAN BEHAN*

Backdrop of Poverty

At 6:30 A.M., while silk-stocking Manhattan is asleep, East Harlem is starting to bustle. The poor are early risers. They have the jobs others don't want: the early-hour jobs, the late-hour jobs. Many rise early because it is a rural habit.

Along about 7:30 the streets are filled with fast-moving people: men, women, and swarms of children of all sizes. The parochial school children can be seen in clusters, with their togetherness identity tag—a school hat, a blouse, a uniform.

You may be able to buy a *New York Times* at the corner newsstand in the morning, but you probably will not be able to buy a cup of coffee. The poor drink their coffee and eat their breakfasts, such as they are, at home. Few eat out.

*The quoted material that the reader will find all through the book is, except where otherwise indicated, excerpted from tape-recorded conversations with individuals and groups of citizens, teachers, youths, and fifth and sixth grade students in East Harlem.

Some will stand at the bus stops, but most will crowd into the downtown subways that speed them to jobs in commercial or silk-stocking areas: to serve the affluent, or work in their stores or small industrial shops. Many of the Negro women will go to domestic service; and the Puerto Rican women, to their sewing machines in the garment shops.

Later in the day, if it is warm, the men who have no jobs will come out and stand on the sidewalks and talk together. They will watch the street and the passers-by and kibitz with one another. The old people, and from time to time the housewives, will sit at the window and join the watchers. And those with leisure may call them idle. Later, when the children return from school, the sidewalks and streets will jump with activity. Clusters of men, sitting on orange crates on the sidewalks, will play checkers or cards. The women will sit on the stoop, arms folded, and watch the young at play; and the young men, flexing their muscles, will look for some adventure. Vendors, ringing their bells, will hawk hot dogs, orange drinks, ice cream; and the caressing but often jarring noise of honking horns, music, children's games, and casual quarrels, whistles, singing, will go on late into the night. When you are in it you don't notice the noise, but when you stand away and listen to a taped conversation, the sound suddenly appears as a background roar. This loud stimulation of the senses may produce some of the emotionalism of the poor.

East Harlem is a busy place, night and day, filled with the joyous and troubled lives of residents—rather than the heavy commercial traffic of mid-Manhattan. New York's street life is unique. So much action, so much togetherness. The critics who lament its passing have a point. The middle class who disdain life conducted so openly in the streets might compare its satisfactions to the sometimes parched and estranged quality of their own backyards.

East Harlem is a land of juveniles, especially in public housing. One of six residents of the area is under thirteen. One of four is under nineteen. As these children grow up and marry they are likely to leave East Harlem, abandoning it to the aged and to new migrants with large families of small children.

The most striking contrast between the rich and the poor areas of Manhattan is in the visible wealth of the one and the visible children of the other. Also, there is the obvious restraint of the one and the expressiveness of the other. In East Harlem, music is everywhere, and visible gaiety, anger, fear, love, hatred.

East Harlem is the poorest spot in one of the richest areas of the world, Manhattan. Across its southern border is the glitter of the east side gold coast, home of some of the world's richest and most celebrated people. On its west flank is another fabled area, Negro Central Harlem, off-and-on home of Adam Clayton Powell, A. Philip Randolph, James Baldwin, Malcolm X, Langston Hughes.

In contrast to such celebrities, East Harlem is plain Jane. If it is "exotic," as advertising for middle income housing claims, that is because of its Spanish flavor below 125th Street. Almost half of its population speaks Spanish. As one of the world's largest Spanish communities, it has been a port of entry for the vast migration that has shuttled back and forth by air express from San Juan to New York for two decades.

The spirited Latin music of East Harlem, pouring out from open tenement windows in every block, is Puerto Rican. Many signs, directions, conversations are in Spanish. The culture, the dark and tight style of dress, and the way of life, the store front pentecostal churches, the pleasantness and gentleness are among Puerto Rico's contributions to East Harlem.

East Harlem is special. Even the schools are special. They are tooled up with knowledge of the Puerto Rican language and culture, as they never were for other migrants. And the older groups say that the Puerto Ricans are coddled: "They never did it for us."

Italians, from an earlier immigration wave, and increasingly

Negroes, who fill up the places not occupied by the Puerto Ricans, add other dimensions to the culture.

East Harlem is special because, except for a number of small Puerto Rican *bodegas*, it has few of Manhattan's accessories: gathering places, commerce, quaint little stores, office buildings, hotels. It is rather like a barracks, a place of residence for some 180,000 people—who populate a community big enough to call itself a city.

PRELUDE

In East Harlem the present emerges from a rich past. Though much of the culture of earlier generations, as well as most historical landmarks, have given way to succeeding waves of immigrants and been torn up by bulldozers, the past is still visible in East Harlem's streets. Peeling off the layers of East Harlem's history reveals a skeleton outline of the nation's past—the swift change from rural to urban and the breathless turnover of ethnic groups.

In the mid-1600s, northern Manhattan was a Dutch colony used for trade with the Indians. By 1661 some thirty-two families lived there, farming the land, quarreling with the Indians, and building a stockade for protection. In 1660 the first church went up at 125 Street and the Harlem river.

In 1685 Dutch Governor Stuyvesant offered one clergyman to any twenty-five families establishing a village in the northern part of the island. When the village was set up, with its quota of clerics, it was called New Haarlem after Haarlem in Holland. By 1779 the Dutch were long gone and Harlem was almost deserted of inhabitants. In 1783 Washington marched on Harlem, then took possession of the city from the British. During the next fifty years Harlem became a retreat for sportsmen and an area of private estates.

In 1816 the common council appropriated $400 for the purchase of land for Harlem's first school. By 1845 there were four schools in upper East Harlem. By the 1850s, 125 Street, one of Harlem's main thoroughfares, had become an exclusive residential street. A lot on Fifth Avenue and 125 Street was worth $1,000—compared with $600 for a lot on 117 Street, and $100 for a lot farther east.

In 1837 the Harlem railroad had opened, making the area accessible to the rest of New York, and by 1887 the Second and Third Avenue elevateds operated to 129 Street. In 1904 the first subway was built, from Brooklyn Bridge to 145 Street and Broadway. The Harlem of the 1880s was mainly a village of huts for tenants and spacious estates for the wealthy, with the aristocracy living on Pleasant Avenue, and sportsmen using the estates for hunting and horse racing. Much of East Harlem was a Roosevelt family farm.

Apparently the first Negroes came to Harlem in 1890, after housing built on 135 Street could not be rented to whites.

At the beginning of this century, East Harlem was mainly German and Irish. Italians had begun to settle in the 1890s, first on 113 Street and Second Avenue; and by 1910 the Italian immigration was so vast that it had become the second largest group in East Harlem. The Jewish immigrants began arriving in the late nineteenth century, escaping persecution in Russia, and ran neck and neck with the Italian entry to East Harlem. In 1919 the construction of the Lexington Avenue subway drove the last of the well-to-do from East Harlem, though many of their once elegant homes still stand.

To accommodate the mass influx of indigent Italians and Jews, cheap railroad flats were built, lacking sunlight in the interior rooms, and offering only the kitchen sink and kitchen tub for bathing. Roofs and fire escapes offered playgrounds for children and fresh air for adults, and movement was restricted by the need to climb four and five flights of stairs. The railroad flats are still East Harlem's slums.

In 1902–1903, the *First Report of the Tenement House Commission of the City of New York* said: "The uptown side of 108th St. between Second and Third Avenues is really an eye-

sore. The houses are leased and sub-leased with sordid specula-
tion, not to say more, a circumstance that precludes all attempts
on the part of the leasee to make repairs without being com-
pelled to do so by the department, and this is the reason the rag-
dealers and peddlers have found their quarters in this block." A
middle income cooperative, Franklin Plaza, has replaced this
block of tenements, but many others remain.

During World War I business boomed in East Harlem, and
the Italians and others took to making goods that could not be
imported. Large homes were converted to sweatshops, employing Italian women and children for the production of em-
broidery. After the war, industry and population began to
decrease. By the late 1920s, Germans had virtually disappeared
from East Harlem. Italians and Jews were also beginning to
move out, and the Puerto Ricans to move in. Negroes too were
moving over from Central Harlem. So the community we know
today took shape.

2

*The trouble is that there is—like a Negro
restaurant—and they won't let the white people
in. And if the white people have a restaurant
they won't let the Negro people in. Suppose I'm
big and I have a restaurant, I let everybody
come in. If they don't disturb me and they
don't have no fights, I let them come in. They
could be welcome. I know a lot of Negro
people, and they're one of my best friends,
and they never act tough like some people do.*
—A SIXTH GRADE PUERTO RICAN GIRL

Neighbors—Puerto Rican, Negro, Italian

East Harlem cuts deep into Manhattan, on two square miles of
the highest priced rock in the world, running from the East
River to Central Park, and roughly from 96 to 130 Streets on
Manhattan's east side.

Its borders are always shifting. So are its neighborhoods, or
subareas. Some have their own identity. When the European
immigrants dominated East Harlem they referred to it as "the
neighborhood." It was then more a neighborhood simply transferred from some European town to the New World, with the
same people and the same culture. Though Italians still talk
about "the neighborhood," social workers and the new migrants
—Puerto Ricans and Negroes—know that physical togetherness
alone does not make people neighbors.

The community is divided, says a City Planning Commission
report, into several social areas. A commuter's railroad track on

7

Park Avenue, the former site of an elevated line, a hill on 102 Street are natural borders that create subareas. These may, like national boundaries, isolate one group from another and give rise to separate patterns of living. Often the borders separate the more from the less desirable areas.

Public housing can be a more formidable barricade than streets, tracks, and lines of transportation. The giant projects tend, like barbed wire, to shut off communications. Projects midway in East Harlem stretch across its whole width and cut it in two. To the north and west of this barrier are the dominantly Negro neighborhoods. To the south on one end is El Barrio, the oldest Puerto Rican settlement in the states.

Mixed in with El Barrio's Spanish residents are some West Indians, Irish, Russians, Hungarians, and Negroes. Its nerve center is the enclosed market under the Park Avenue railroad tracks. Here goods and information are exchanged. Some claim that prostitution and the narcotics trade are rife in El Barrio, on 110 and 111 Streets, for example, west of Park Avenue. Two active community groups also work there: the Taft Neighborhood Development Committee and the East Harlem Reform Democrats. Along Fifth Avenue and in a different world is a towering row of public institutions facing Fifth Avenue and Central Park, their backs turned to the slum.

The "Triangle" at the northern end of East Harlem between 125 and 130 Streets is probably Harlem's poorest spot. Though it has a number of stable residents, its present, predominantly Negro population includes many recent arrivals from the rural Deep South. It stands in a corner by itself, isolated, ignored by many agencies that tend to the southern tier. The Triangle is the end of the line for many hard-core cases. The bulldozers have pushed them about, like gravel, from one spot to another, and now they are here, many of them too down-and-out to qualify for public housing. Again the bulldozers may push them out. The next step in their line of march seems to be the East River.

Better a neighbor that is near than a brother far off.

—PROVERBS

East Harlem is now brimming with a mixture of dark and volatile people: Puerto Ricans who give it a Spanish accent (41 per cent), Negroes (38 per cent), Italians and others (21 per cent).

The most significant recent population change is the increase in Negro residents. Many of them came in with the new public housing projects. In 1940 Negroes were only 20 per cent of East Harlem's population. In each recent decade Negroes increased by roughly 10 per cent. As in other cities, New York City's Negro population has been dispersing. The increase of Negro population now comes mainly from natural increase rather than new migration. The migrations have merely slowed, not stopped, and newcomers in undetermined numbers still arrive from the most backward rural areas of Puerto Rico and the deepest South.

Puerto Ricans have also increased. They were only 30 per cent of the total in 1950. The Italians, until recently dominant, are still leaving for Long Island and other suburban points. Both East and Central Harlem have been losing population very rapidly. East Harlem's loss was 17 per cent in the 1960 census. Central Harlem's was about 14 per cent, most of it in the 21 to 44 age group. The young grow up and leave when they marry and start work.

East Harlem's residents have known upheaval and change. About half of its population moved from one place to another during one five-year period. In Central Harlem only one out of three moved.

Woe unto him that is alone when he falleth.

—ECCLESIASTES

Cultural differences have been rather overplayed in discussions of the disadvantaged. Idiosyncracies of culture are of more interest and use to the tourist than to the advocate of progress and change. What is most significant about the culture of the disadvantaged is that its essentials are much like those of the advantaged, minus the material comforts and self-respect that are their by-products. A brief tour of East Harlem's culture, here and later in the book, will suffice, with a pause for a taste of its special Puerto Rican flavor.

"The cultural attitudes of the Puerto Rican and Negro segments toward authority are in direct contradiction to each other," Preston Wilcox observed as director of the East Harlem Project. Puerto Ricans tended "to be submissive toward authority and thus easily came under the domination of a single leader who did little to develop their potential. The Negro segment tended to be aggressive toward authority—the result being that they continued to receive 'guarded' reactions from authority figures with little goal achievement."*

Submission from one group, aggression from the other; neither gets the most out of authority. Puerto Ricans, it is claimed, favor the "maximal leader," the unquestioned leader that all follow: a corollary in everyday life is that "If they like you, they'll accept anything from you." Protest leaders in East Harlem are critical of Puerto Ricans for accepting social inequities and for their "failure to join Negroes in protest." It is said that Puerto Ricans are "more American than Americans," and that anything in the United States goes with them; they do not complain.

An estimated one-fourth of Puerto Ricans are Negro. Though Puerto Ricans tend to be racially unbiased, by mainland standards, the dark-skinned Puerto Ricans say they are treated as the "lowest" in their families, and it is said that the Puerto Rican drug addict is almost always the darkest member of his family.

Though conflict is still open, Puerto Ricans are closer in life

* Preston Wilcox, "Grassroots Participation, a Step Toward Better Mental Health," *Realizing the Mental Health Potentials for Children and Youth in City Living.* Proceedings of a conference held by the Manhattan Society for Mental Health, October 2–4, 1961, p. 46.

style, religion, and attitudes to their Italian rather than their Negro neighbors. Italians, an exclusive and "cornered" community in East Harlem, accept neither group, but Puerto Ricans are less rejected and some intergroup dating and marriage do occur. Only a few Puerto Ricans and even fewer Negroes are to be seen in the Italian's last major preserve: La Guardia Neighborhood House. A mixed dance was once held there (Italian and Puerto Rican), but the boys fought over mixed couple dancing, and the attempt at friendship through youth socializing was all but abandoned. La Guardia House still sponsors a fairly active Italian–Puerto Rican friendship group (which Negroes say should include them too) to reduce violent conflict and help in neighborhood improvement.

All three groups are fond of music and dancing. While the Puerto Rican youth retain much of their "folk music," the Italian youth are almost submerged in the pop music of the larger "youth culture" and rarely speak Italian or sing Italian songs in public.

Sex is a favorite subject if not activity, though strong restraints on girls are found among Italians and Puerto Ricans. One youth worker, who has lived or worked in East Harlem all his life, claimed that "all the kids can think of is sex"; he referred to all three ethnic groups. "No wonder they can't learn anything in school," he said, "they have sex on their mind 24 hours a day."

One teacher described her Puerto Rican and Negro children as "very active" physically. "They love to dance and move their bodies. They can't sit still. The ones that do well in school usually don't like to dance or move around. When I had a group to my house, they all danced wildly, except one girl who was the best student in the school. She didn't dance at all."

"The children here," she said, "can do so much on their own —sewing, and painting, and creative work. The middle class children always have to be taken care of. They want you to do everything for them." East Harlem's children tend to take on responsibility and independence at an early age, and to "do for themselves."

Teachers and others claim that Puerto Ricans keep their children close to home and off the streets, while the Negro children are permitted much more freedom of the streets and sidewalks. Puerto Rican girls, in particular, are closely watched and sheltered, and are rarely permitted out at night without an adult escort. This restriction is breaking down with time. Italian girls too are very closely watched by their parents, and many are continually in trouble with parents about keeping late hours or not being home on time. Negro girls are given much more freedom.

While Italian youths express open and profound racist feelings, Puerto Ricans, themselves a racial mixture, tend to feel that "everyone is equal" and that they should not talk against Negroes. Some, in unguarded moments, will express fear of Negroes. One sixth grader said: "The Negro people, they all act tough. The colored people, if we walk down the street and if a Negro were walking by and we looked at them, they just start a fight. If we're walking down the street, my grandmother says, and I see a Negro walking down the street, he could talk anything he want, I would look down not to see his face because the Negro people act tough. They say 'what are you looking at?' "

Their relations are better with Spanish Negroes: "Where I used to go there was some nice Negro people. I used to always be with them and take them to my house and give them candy or anything what I had. I had a friend, she was real nice with me. She used to always, you know, stick with me, and another girl named Margie, you know, she was colored people. Colored, yeah, but she was Spanish, she was just like me. She lived in the same building and we three used to always stick together. I think sometime that Negro people are generous too."

The dark-skinned Puerto Rican child tastes mainland racial prejudice and doesn't like it at all; it helps him understand, however, what American Negroes have to live with. A sixth grade Puerto Rican girl tells this story of discovery:

I went to Lane's about two weeks before Easter, and I looked all over the place, and my mother is light skinned and I was with her. So I looked all over the place like that and I didn't see nobody my color and I said to my mother, "I'll wait out here," and she said, "No, you come in here." We went up to the top part to find the hats, so I got on the escalator and there was these light-skinned people on the escalator going down and I was going up and they were looking at me and I had this badge that said about the Beatles "I like Paul," and they looked at me, and this lady stuck her tongue out at me. And I asked my mother and my mother said, "You don't live with her, keep walking," but they were all looking at me and I thought because I was the only dark-skin in there. I looked all over the place and I was the only one dark skin.

Race and ethnicity underlie much of the open and hidden conflict in East Harlem, as it always has in the slums of New York's melting pot. The poor, consumed by conflict with the new poor who are moving in on top of them, often ignore "enemies without" and those at a distance who pull the strings that manipulate their lives.

Typically, in the old tenement housing, these groups will not live together in the same building, though they may live in adjacent buildings or at opposite ends of a block. In the new public housing projects, they at least share the same roof, however little they may communicate under it. In the old blocks, one side of the street may be Italian and the other side Puerto Rican. The melting down of these new migrants, the effort of learning to talk and share and work together, is a slow and troubled process.

Politically, the Puerto Ricans in East Harlem have tended to form alliances with Negroes rather than with Italians within the Democratic party, and they have now successfully taken over much of the party's control from the Italians.

The rapidly diminishing Italian community tends to live in

the old row houses rather than the projects; a number of Italians are home owners who are aging and want to stay in their old neighborhood. Italian youths of dating age are boxed in, constrained from dating Puerto Ricans and Negroes, and unable to find a big enough matrimonial field in their own community; Irish boys from other neighborhoods are desirable to the girls but not very accessible. The Italians are more prosperous than the other groups and the Puerto Ricans least prosperous. Negroes tend to favor project living, and they now constitute a fairly large upwardly mobile and unusually sophisticated group in East Harlem, though there are also large numbers of destitute people.

The Italian community is tightly sealed against outsiders; many of East Harlem's "Italians" are Sicilians, some of whom have been (some claim still are) close to the Sicilian underworld; nobody talks about it to outsiders. This underworld may have been, in fact, East Harlem's most earnest "self-help" effort —a community project that serviced people in a variety of legal and illegal ways, gave assistance, welfare, and protection, enriched some and helped others rise out of poverty. Neither Puerto Ricans nor Negroes have had any comparable organization.

> *I have shut my balcony*
> *because I do not want to hear the lament,*
> *but from behind the grey walls*
> *I hear nothing else but the lament.*
> —GARCIA LORCA

The gray poverty of the old Spanish section of East Harlem, roughly marked by 96 and 112 Streets on the south and north and Fifth and Third Avenues on the west and east, contrasts with the green poverty of the homeland, Puerto Rico.

The island, once a U.S. colony, is now a commonwealth. It elects its own government and pays no taxes to the United States. Yet it receives the benefits of U.S. citizenship and limited

U.S. federal services and funds. Recent economic growth has made it the most prosperous Latin American territory, though it is still a long way from prosperity as we know it.

The Puerto Rican migration to *Nueva York*, unchecked by immigrant quotas, is a major source of the island's prosperity. It upgraded the migrants, converted them from rural to urban people, relieved the island of some of its labor surplus, and sent lots of cash back home.

The commonwealth government plays many improvisations on the mixed economy theme. It built much of the industry on the island and still operates some of it. It also gives substantial tax exemptions to private enterprises that have been brought in from the states, and feverishly encourages private investment.

In Puerto Rico the outsider is aware of a national spirit amid residual poverty. A spirit that is busy and buzzing and wide-eyed rather than shrewd, ruthless, competitive. It is a lyric and a creative excitement rather than a highly organized or mechanized one. Many people, very modest people, seem to think it is their job to do something: first for their people, second for themselves. It seems the reverse of what they run into in New York City. The rural *campesinos* are still impoverished, however, and 13 per cent of the labor force is unemployed.

For an industrializing people, many Puerto Ricans have an incongruous bubbling of good spirits. Mainland visitors usually love the island and wonder why Puerto Ricans left this lovely place to live in El Barrio.

The simple answer of course is poverty. They left in search of a job, food, good shoes, a phonograph, a chance to succeed—just like everyone else. New York is cold and gray; Puerto Rico is green and warm, an island paradise. It is so close to New York by air coach that Puerto Ricans continue to have some of the best of two worlds and, unlike any previous migrants, keep one foot in the green homeland and the other in gray El Barrio or south Bronx.

The migration to New York City, where 60 per cent of the

migrants (over 650,000) came is said to have stopped.* It is harder to get jobs in the states and easier for those with skills to get jobs in the island than before. So many return to their "rich port" or never leave in the first place. Some learn skills on the mainland and go home to use them, or acquire capital and go home to set up a business.

Meanwhile Puerto Ricans helped those back home. In 1954, $3 million went from New York to Puerto Rico by postal money order alone. In 1940 bank deposits in Puerto Rico were $76 million; in 1961, $674 million. About half the capital invested in new manufacturing now comes from Puerto Rico itself. Political power has changed hands. Once dominated by sugar lawyers, the legislature came to be heavily influenced by labor leaders and spokesmen. It is this political change that produced economic change. The great Governor Luis Muñoz himself was influenced by the U.S. labor movement, as were many of the new Puerto Rican leaders.

In the 1930s, after some thirty-five years of American colonial status, Puerto Rico was impoverished, illiterate, diseased, congested. About one-third of all births were illegitimate. It was almost wholly dependent on sugar and had little industry. In other words, it resembled most of Latin America. With its commonwealth status came new life and prosperity.

In El Barrio and New York generally, about half of adult Puerto Ricans are disqualified from voting by English literacy tests. Most are literate and could pass tests in Spanish, but not English. The Puerto Rican's political disfranchisement greatly weakens his organized strength in New York.

Nominally Roman Catholic, about ten times as many Puerto

---

* About 50,000 Puerto Ricans are going north each year, but there has in the past few years been a great increase in the number returning. The return migration went up to 33,000 in 1963 and is expected to be over 50,000 in 1964.

In 1960 Puerto Rican per capita income was just below $700 a year, the highest in Latin America, but less than half that of Mississippi.

Of new professional jobs created in Puerto Rico between 1955 and 1960 (3,000), 28 per cent were taken by returned migrants. Of 6,000 new merchant and commercial openings, 36 per cent were filled by returnees.

Rican children go to public as to parochial school, though the New York archdiocese has about 250 Spanish-speaking priests. There are some 4,000 Puerto Rican-run businesses in New York.

El Diario—La Prensa, a Spanish daily paper in New York that prints Puerto Rican news, is owned by Roy Chalk, of Trans-Caribbean Airways, a non-Puerto Rican. The paper is called the "patron" of many Puerto Ricans; some say it is a Puerto Rican equivalent of Tammany Hall. Others criticize its "conservatism" and influence on Puerto Rican opinion.

Some Puerto Ricans have moved up rather fast in New York. In 1950, only 24 per cent of mainland-born Puerto Rican women were in sales and clerical occupations. A decade later, 43 per cent held these jobs.

Many Puerto Rican women marry and bear children while *they* are still children. The birth rate for girls younger than 20 is *five times* higher among Puerto Ricans and Negroes than among non-Puerto Rican white groups. The effect of the combination of large families and low wages is visible in the ethnic make-up of the New York City Welfare Department's recipients of supplementary assistance, assistance given those who have jobs but whose wages do not cover their minimum needs. One-half of all families in New York who receive this assistance are Puerto Rican. Thus government subsidizes the hundreds of marginal businesses in the city that do not pay a living wage.

Birth control is a big issue with Puerto Ricans, as it is with others. The women so want to keep down family size, says Elena Padilla, in her book *Up from Puerto Rico,** that "abortions and other forms of discontinuing pregnancies may be attempted," such as castor oil, quinine pills, strong purgatives and teas. Abortions, carried out by women (*comandronas*) who do them for small fees, "are closely guarded secrets, for, reported one informant, 'a woman who has an abortion can be sentenced to death in the electric chair.' " Sterilization, obtained

* New York, Columbia University Press, 1958.

without great difficulty in Puerto Rico, is said to be preferred to contraception.

Many Puerto Ricans, she reports, regard other Puerto Ricans as "worthless" because of their "lack of unity" and because in New York they do not "help each other as they do in Puerto Rico."

"Americans" are highly regarded by Puerto Ricans. They are said to be "nice, honest, beautiful, and funny." "Americans," as defined by Puerto Ricans, are nonimmigrant whites. The second-generation New York Puerto Ricans interviewed gave a "high" rating to Americans, Cubans, Italian, Jewish and other European immigrants; a "medium" rating to American Negroes including West Indians; and a *"low" rating to the new Puerto Rican migrant.* "For some Hispanos it is openly accepted and unquestioned that Hispanos are undesirable persons." One Puerto Rican voiced his feelings when he said, "Our race, the Latin race, has spoiled this country by the use of drugs. That is why the Americans hate us."

Such feelings are not usually reciprocated. Only American Negroes, West Indians, and Cubans rated Puerto Ricans "high." Italians rated them "medium." Others rated them "low."

Though Puerto Ricans are a mixed race, ranging from blonde to black, the "mainsprings of intergroup tensions in the neighborhood lie between recent Puerto Rican migrants and American Negroes." Puerto Ricans speak of Negroes as "bad, dangerous, and capable of violence against them." The Negroes and Puerto Ricans who have lived in the neighborhood for years however "have learned to associate with each other in small groups, become close friends, visit each other, and share in real comradeship."

In East Harlem the beginnings of a close alliance between Negro and Puerto Rican can be seen, but there is still tension and fear. Many Puerto Rican and Negro parents keep their small children close to home or inside the apartment even in hot summer months. The streets are dangerous, they say; they are filled with youths whose parents do not try or cannot keep them home; they are filled with young men who are too old to be told what to do and who, in their tragic idleness, have a way of teaching "bad things" to the young or getting in trouble with other ethnic groups.

Among Puerto Ricans the family is stressed as the "center of an adult's obligations," while individuality and "doing things just for oneself are discouraged as being of no value."

Success and achievement are encouraged only as ways to help the family. The person who does not succeed can expect help from the family. As one person put it: "A good life is when we work and we have the things we need for all the family." Independence and self-reliance "are not to be encouraged in a child." Good children are defined as "obedient, respectful, and docile."

For recent migrants, prized values are: being a "good" worker, formal schooling, learning English while not forgetting Spanish, desiring "progress" and getting ahead ("get the feet off the dish") especially through the education of children, not letting anyone "take you for a ride," being quiet, being careful in choosing friends, and trusting only a few people.

It is considered "an essential quality of a good and worthwhile person that he "have sentiment." Women may express grief by an "attack"—loud screaming, shaking, falling to the floor with arms rigidly extended and hands clenched. Attacks are regarded as a "demonstration of intense grief and great affection for the person in danger." A man is not criticized for crying or having an "ataque."

In El Barrio, says a City Planning Commission report, Puerto Ricans "are extraordinarily gregarious and have greatly suffered the loss of the small shop. The *bodega*, the barber shop, the small Puerto Rican luncheonette and the township club were and are, in the cases of the few remaining ones, the meeting grounds for Puerto Ricans of all ages."

As a group they would rather take "every precaution to hide

and shelter a relative for years than reveal the exact number of occupants in an apartment to a building inspector or landlord."

One young Negro, president of a public housing tenant council in El Barrio, complained that Puerto Ricans are hard to talk to about tenant meetings.

"Fear is everything," he said. "It's the only thing that works. I used to go to their door and they'd close it in my face. Now I canvass with a Puerto Rican fellow and they talk to him. He goes to the door and says: 'Do you want to be shot? Do you want to be robbed? If you don't, you'd better support the tenant's council—because we're going to get rid of crime around here. Otherwise, there's no telling what will happen to you.' He signs them up."

Up farther, in the Triangle, organizers say the few Puerto Ricans there are much easier to organize than Negroes and much less afraid. Perhaps Puerto Ricans living in slum housing are less afraid and feel less strange than those living in new projects.

El Barrio's streets and life are tied into the blood stream of the city. They are not detachable. Many people do not seem to have this clearly enough in mind; East Harlem seems to them almost a separate duchy, which can go it alone.

Even less clear, and further from view, is the connection of the community with the state and federal systems. In these distant centers most of the strings are pulled that manipulate the lives of slum dwellers.

The neglect of the slum, and discrimination against it, come out of the city's neglect by the state and federal systems. The city, and increasingly its suburbs, stand against the state system, which is controlled by rural and business interests. And, when the "state system" and its political conservatism control the federal system, the city stagnates and suffers. It is always in need of massive transfusions from the federal system. Its own money-raising powers are limited by the state, and contributions from anticity state legislatures are not generous.

Neglect of the city has spawned East Harlem's slums. It has produced massive pathology in the whole city. The wounds of East Harlem and El Barrio will probably never heal while the city's sores are raw.

3

I like Long Island, good houses, and the parents are better. Right here you see them take numbers, and they drink a lot. Sometimes I get angry, and I always say I'm going to run away from home. Then sometimes I say, "Well, where am I going to sleep? Where am I going to eat and all that?" Then I say, "How could I be a scientist if I don't go to school or nothing like that." I start to bother my sister. My mother comes. Sometimes she hits me. I get angry. I say I'm going to run away tonight. I wake up in the middle of the night. I'm ready to leave, and then I say, "Should I stay or shouldn't I?" And I go back to sleep.

—AN ELEVEN-YEAR-OLD PUERTO RICAN BOY

New York's Lower Depths

But is the whole of East Harlem a slum? In its low income housing projects, families on welfare range from 13 per cent in one to 21 per cent in another. Still, the majority of families are self-supporting.

The Triangle is an American Casbah, loaded with troubles and despair, but even there can be found much hope. In the Triangle's thirty-six acres, more than half the families are stable enough to have lived there for from eleven to twenty-one years. In a study done by a local group, 15 per cent of the residents were found to have criminal records and 10 per cent to be narcotics addicts. The reverse is that even in this trouble spot only a small minority were addicted and relatively few had criminal records.

On a warm summer day the broken and derelict men are visible on the Triangle streets, sodden with despair and whatever they take to make their internal escape from the slum. But far more numerous at some hours of the day are the spirited and attractive young men and women. While some of the Triangle's citizens look sullen and resentful, many do not. No stereotype fits; and, what outsiders would call a slum, many insiders would not.

One young Puerto Rican described East Harlem this way: "I'm 23 years old, and I've been living here all my life. I never been out of this neighborhood. To me this neighborhood is all right. People who have money—maybe it's a dump, as they call it, but this is my home." It is not a slum to everyone.

The relevant facts about East Harlem's poverty were turned up by a mayor's study. They showed that one in five New Yorkers lives in conditions of poverty. Though more than half of the poor are white, nonwhites are 29 per cent of the poor and Puerto Ricans 19 per cent. The poor are largely confined to sixteen of the seventy-four recognized communities of the city —one of them East Harlem, the poorest of the poor.

Nothing more meaningful about East Harlem can be found than the fact that its median family income of $3,700 is $2,300 a year lower than the median for the city, or that jobless rates for Negroes run about 50 per cent above the norm of whites and for Puerto Ricans about 100 per cent.

About half of all private dwellings in East Harlem are dilapidated. Almost one in three is overcrowded. It is possible that crowding alone may produce much of the slum's stress. Experimental biologist Dr. Hudson Hoagland has found that overcrowding in animal society can produce stress-induced maladies —liver disease, heart trouble, sexual deviation—that serve as natural population controls. When crowded, animals die off despite adequate food; rats show abnormal sexual and social behavior. It is part of the "acute stress syndrome," he suggests, that results from the overactivity of the pituitary adrenal system, which regulates the release of hormones during stress.

Slum dwellers may be reacting in the same physiological way

as the biologist's animals. Most people need and want privacy, at least on occasion—a room of one's own, an escape from family demands, noise, conflict. Because of the continuing bombardment of the senses, day and night, many slum children wake up nervous and tired. But the children are not lonely, and they are less likely than the more isolated "only child" of the middle class family to commit suicide.

A Negro woman in East Harlem expressed a common opinion: "We're in such crowded tenements down here, that it's hard to live privately. Your neighbors can't move—because of the salaries that are being made—into a decent neighborhood. The mix is good. You have to mix in order to get along with people. But the living *so close together*, that's a bit too much."

In East Harlem tuberculosis rates are high and venereal disease (VD) rates are more than twice the city average. Crowding helps spread disease. So does the inability of the poor to pay for decent medical care.*

Crowded rooms and lack of privacy no doubt help persuade East Harlem's youths (indeed the poor everywhere) to marry younger than do their middle class peers. Since the young are even less able to buy medical care, *one out of three pregnant mothers gets no prenatal attention*. Not surprisingly then, infant mortality is 37 per 1,000 live births (compared with the city average of 26), and 50 per cent of the infant deaths occur on the first day of life.

The typical East Harlem resident has never been to high school. Median school years finished are 8.2. Only one out of five has graduated from high school. Only one out of twenty has had any college. Of all residents in upper Manhattan who have had no formal education, 50 per cent live in East Harlem, and most are Puerto Ricans.

* More than 90 per cent of East Harlem school children depend on institutional medical care. New York's Health Commissioner, Dr. George James, said that "poverty is the third leading cause of death" in the city. He attributes 13,000 deaths a year to it, including cancer, diabetes, pneumonia, influenza, cardiovascular diseases, and accidents, along with tuberculosis and VD.

In East Harlem few residents (and those mainly Italians) own their own homes. By contrast, nationally 38 per cent of Negroes and 64 per cent of whites in 1960 owned their own homes.*

The typical New Yorker is a tenant. As such he is denied the status, power, and stability that the American's chief property assets can offer: a home and the car that usually goes in its garage. The New Yorker, the poorer one in particular, typically has neither. Many like it this way and prefer apartment living when there are no young children in their families. But it is not clear what the effect the total denial of these assets has on the poor and others. The lack of these major creative and recreational outlets may result in significant psychological deprivation. Though caring for a house and car is simply a chore for many middle class people, manual workers often find in it a major source of satisfaction. If a worker is handy with his hands he will spend much of his time with his house and car, finishing the basement or attic, building a fence or porch, repairing his car. Do-it-yourself attitudes and skills are by-products of car and home ownership. So is the sense of control over the environment and the machine. It is a vital part of the American style of life that is missing in East Harlem and other rental areas. If the residents of East Harlem owned these buildings they would not permit them to remain in their present state of decay. They would be moved to clean, paint, and fix. As it is they think it is the landlord's responsibility—and almost always it is. In the rental slums of New York, apartment ownership may offer a substitute for home ownership.

In other cities, even the poor, unless they are desperate, often buy their homes if only on land contract. In New York the poor rent. As renters they usually contend with absentee landlords, who neglect their property. The tenants complain. The

* The typical owner-occupied Negro home was valued at $6,700 in 1960, compared to $12,230 for the white home. In 1950, 35 per cent of Negroes and 57 per cent of whites owned their homes; thus the rate of increase has been greater for whites.

landlords ignore them. The city investigates; nothing happens. Tenants are helpless, unable to move either landlords or the city to action. Since a serious housing shortage still exists in the city, they are unable to move out to better housing.

RENT STRIKE

> *My days are swifter than a weaver's shuttle, and are*
> *spent without hope.*
>
> —JOB

It was natural that the rent strike, one of the most potent (if controversial and short-lived) direct action devices New York's poor have found, should have begun inside East Harlem.

The Community Council on Housing, led by Jesse Gray, had its offices in East Harlem. One of the first buildings struck was 16 East 117 Street, in East Harlem, owned by a matron living in Teaneck, New Jersey. After the strike began in this building, the landlord tried to dispossess the tenants. The court, inspecting building violations, ordered the rent paid to the court rather than the landlord. Later the city started receivership proceedings, and the rent money was returned to the tenants.

Mrs. Inocencia Flores, Apartment 3W, was among the striking tenants. Born in Puerto Rico, where she attended high school and for a time the University of Puerto Rico, she came to New York in 1944 and began work in the garment district, trimming and making clothes. At the time of the strike, she had four children, was on relief, and separated from her husband.

Her diary, kept while her building was on strike, tells part of her story.*

Wednesday, Feb. 5: I got up at 6:45. The first thing to do was light the oven. The boiler was broke so not getting the heat. All the tenants together bought the oil. We give $7.50 for each tenant. But the boiler old and many things we don't know about the pipes, so one of the men next door who used to be superintendent is try-

---

* Francis Sugrue, "Diary of a Rent Striker," *New York Herald Tribune,* February 16, 1964, p. 28.

ing to fix. I make the breakfast for the three children who go to school. I give them orange juice, oatmeal, scrambled eggs, and Ovaltine. They have lunch in school and sometimes they don't like the food and won't eat, so I say you have a good breakfast. Miss Christine Washington stick her head in at 7:30 and say she go to work. I used to live on ground floor and she was all the time trying to get me move to third floor next door to her because this place vacant and the junkies use it and she scared the junkies break the wall to get into her place and steal everything because she live alone and go to work.

I'm glad I come up here to live because the rats so big downstairs. We all say the "rats is big as cats." I had a baseball bat for the rats. It's lucky me and the children never got bit. The children go to school and I clean the house and empty the pan in the bathroom that catches the water dripping from pipe in the big hole in the ceiling. You have to carry umbrella to the bathroom sometimes. I go to the laundry place this afternoon and I wash again on Saturday because I change my kids clothes every day because I don't want them dirty to attract the rats.

At 12:15 I am fixing lunch for myself and the little one, Tom. I make for him two soft boiled eggs and fried potatoes. He likes catsup and he has one slice of spam and a cup of milk. I have some spam for myself and salad because I only drink a cup of coffee at breakfast because I'm getting too fat. I used to work in the shipping department of bathing suits and the boss used to tell me to model for the buyers. I was a model, but now I'm too fat.

After I go out to a rent strike meeting at night, I come home and the women tell me that five policemen came and broke down the door of the vacant apartment of the ground floor where we have meetings for the tenants in our building. They come looking for something—maybe junkies, but we got nothing in there only paper and some chairs and tables. They knocked them all over. The women heard the policemen laughing. When I come up to my place the children already in bed and I bathe myself and then I go to bed and read the newspaper until 11:30.

Thursday, Feb. 6: I wake up at six o'clock and I went to the kitchen to heat a bottle for my baby. When I put the light on the kitchen I yelled so loud that I don't know if I disturbed the neighbors. There was a big rat coming out from the garbage pail. He looks like a cat. I ran to my room, I called my daughter Carmen to go to the kitchen to see if the coast was clear. She's not scared of the rats. So I could go back to the kitchen to heat the bottle for my baby. Then I left the baby with a friend and went downtown.

Friday, Feb. 7: This morning I woke up a little early. The baby woke up at five o'clock. I went to the kitchen but this time I didn't see the rat.

After the girls left for school I started washing the dishes and cleaning the kitchen. I am thinking about their school. Today they ain't teaching enough. My oldest girl is 5.9 in reading. This is low level in reading. I go to school and English teacher tell me they ain't got enough books to read and that's why my daughter behind. I doesn't care about integration like that. It doesn't bother me. I agree with boycott for some reasons. To get better education and better teachers and better materials in school. I don't like putting them in buses and sending them away. I like to stay here and change the system. Some teachers has to be changed. My girl take Spanish in junior high school, and I said to her, "Tell your teacher I'm going to be in school one day to teach him Spanish because I don't know where he learns to teach Spanish but it ain't Spanish."

I'm pretty good woman. I don't bother anyone. But I got my rights. I fight for them. I don't care about jail. Jail don't scare me. If have to go to jail, I go. I didn't steal. I didn't kill nobody. There's no record for me. But if I have to go, I go.

Saturday, Feb. 8: A tenant called me and asked me what was new in the building because she works daytimes. She wanted to know about the junkies. Have they been on the top floor where the vacant apartments is? That's why I have leaking from the ceiling. The junkies on the top floor break the pipes and take the fixtures and the sink and sell them and that's where the water comes. . . . I'm not ascared of the junkies. I open the door and I see the junkies I tell them to go or I call the police. Many people scared of them, but they scared of my face. I got a baseball bat for the rats and for the junkies. I sometimes see a junkie in the hallway taking the junk and I give him a broom and say "Sweep the hall." And he does what I tell him and hand me back the broom after he sweep the hall. I'm not scared of no junkies. I know my rights and

I know my self-respect. After supper I played cards (casino) for two hours with the girls and later I got dressed and I went to a party for the rent strike. This party was to get funds to the cause. I had a good time. Mr. Gray was there dancing. He was so happy.

Sunday, Feb. 9: I dressed up in a hurry to go to church. When I go to church I pray for to have better house and have a decent living. I hope He's hearing. But I don't get discouraged on Him. I have faith. I don't care how cold I am I never lose my faith. When I come out of church I was feeling so good.

Monday, Feb. 10: At 9:30 a man came to fix the rat holes. He charged me only $3. Then one of the tenants came to tell me that we only had oil for today and every tenant have to give $7.50 to send for more oil. I went to see some tenants to tell them there is no more oil. We all have to cooperate with money for the oil. It's very hard to collect because some are willing to give but others start fussing. I don't know why because is for the benefit of all, especially those with children. We have to be our own landlord and supers. We had to be looking for the building and I tell you we doing better than if there is an owner. Later I went down in the basement with another tenant to see about the boiler, but we found it missing water in the inside and she didn't light it up and anyway there was not too much oil in it. I hope nothing bad happens, because we too had given $5 each tenant to buy some material to repair the boiler. If something happens is going to be pretty hard to make another collection.

Tuesday, Feb. 11: This morning was too cold in the house that I had to light the oven and heat hot water. We had no steam, the boiler is not running good. I feel miserable. You know when the house is cold you can't do nothing. When the girls left for school I went back to bed. I just got up at 11:30 and this house is so cold. Living in a cold apartment is terrible. I wish I could have one of those kerosene stoves to heat myself.

My living room and my room is Alaska. I'm going to heat some pea soup and make coffee. I sat down in the kitchen by the stove to read some papers and keep warm. This is terrible situation. Living the way I live in this slum house is miserable. I don't wish no body to live the way I live. Inside a house in this condition, no steam, no hot water, ceiling falling on you, running water from the ceiling, to go to the bathroom you have to use an umbrella, rats everywhere. I suggest that landlords having human being living this way instead of sending them to jail they must make them live at least a month in this same conditions, so they know the way they pile up money in a bank.

Wednesday, Feb. 12: I wake up around 5 o'clock and the first thing I did was light the oven and the heater so when the girls wake up is a little warm. I didn't call them to 11 because they didn't have to go to school. It still so cold they trembling. You feel like crying looking your children in this way.

I think if I stay a little longer in this kind of living I'm going to be dead duck. I know that to get a project you have to have somebody prominent to back you up. Many people got to the projects and they don't even need them. I had been feeling [filling] applications I don't know since when. This year I feel another one. My only weapon is my vote. This year I *don't vote* for nobody. May be my vote don't count, but don't forget if you have fourteen cent you need another penny so you take the bus or the subway. At least I clean my house and you could eat on the floor. The rest of the day I didn't do nothing. I was so mad all day long. I cooked a big pot of soup. I leave it to God to help me. I have faith in Him.

Thursday, Feb. 13: I couldn't get up this morning. The house was so cold that I came out of bed at 7:15. I heated some water I leave the oven light up all night because the heater gave up. I fixed some oatmeal, eggs and some Ovaltine for the girls. I had some coffee. I clean the house. The baby was sleeping. Later on, the inspector came. They were suppose to come to every apartment and look all violations. They knock at the door and asked if anything had been fixed. I think even the inspectors are afraid of this slum conditions thats why they didn't dare to come inside. I don't blame them. They don't want to take a rat or any bug to their houses, or get dirty in this filthy houses. My little girl come from school with Valentine she made for me. Very pretty. At 8:30 I went downstairs to a meeting we had. We discuss about why there is no heat. We agreed to give $10 to fix the boiler for the oil. A man is coming to fix it. I hope everybody give the $10 so we have some heat soon.

Friday, Feb. 14: I didn't write this about Friday in my book until this Saturday morning, because Friday night I sick and so cold I go to bed and could not write in the book. But this about Friday. I got up at five and light the oven and put some water to heat. At seven I called the two oldest girls for school. I didn't send the little one, because she was coughing too much and with a running nose. I gave some baby aspirin and I put some Vick in her nose and chest and I gave some hot tea. I leaved her in bed.

It was so cold in here that I didn't want to do nothing in the house. I fixed some soup for lunch and read for a while in the kitchen and after a while I went out and clean the hallway. I didn't mop because there was no hot water, but at least the hallway looked a little clean.

Later on I fixed dinner I was not feeling good. I had a headache and my throat hurt. I hope I do not catch a cold. I hope some day God help me and all this experience I had be restore with a very living and happiness. It is really hard to believe that this happens here in New York and richest city in the world. But such is Harlem and hope. Is this the way to live. I rather go to the Moon in the next trip.

The building at 16 East 117 Street is one of 43,000 old-law tenements in New York City, which house about 900,000 people, a population the size of Baltimore, the nation's sixth largest city. Most old-law tenements, particularly those used by generations of poor and transient tenants, are not fit to live in and not economic to renovate. On the other hand, many old buildings, brownstones, and others, are often suitable for tenants or rehabilitation. Welfare Commissioner James Dumpson has said it will take fifty years to meet the housing needs of the city's welfare population alone at present construction rates, and another 100 years to house all the poor. By then the buildings that are habitable now will be in decay.*

In the building on 117 Street, decay set in after a fast shuffle of owners who didn't care and often could not be located: "The superintendent was replaced by a handy man. Then the handy

* In New York City, according to the 1960 census, there are 2,758,419 housing units, and of these 427,572 are classified as "dilapidated or deteriorating."

man was made to be handy in so many places that he became handy in none. When the bell system failed, it was left unrepaired; when the lock was broken, the front door stood open. Tenants endured broken windows, falling plaster, peeling paint, leaking pipes, cracked sinks and toilets, clogged drains, rotten window frames, jammed doors, unlighted halls, unswept stairs, winter days and nights without heat. Then too, there were rats. Traps were set and poisons laid out, but, though some of the rats were caught and some wandered off to die in the walls, a population established itself and fattened and bred on the trash that wasn't collected and the garbage left out in the halls."*

None of the many owners of the house applied to raise rents under the law that guarantees landlords a fair return of at least 6 per cent on investment, plus 2 per cent for depreciation. Apparently the landlords made profits in excess of this legal guarantee.

A group of enterprising women from the Women's City Club of New York, instead of folding bandages or sponsoring talks on poverty, set out to learn for themselves what the slums are like. They chose a block of relatively "good" housing in East Harlem where the "decay of completely neglected slum areas was absent." In 59 apartments they found 1,319 violations of the housing code and unattended decay everywhere. (Their report is summarized in Appendix 1.)

STRIKE GENESIS

The protector of the tenement is less the inspectors than the judges. Courts seldom convict landlords or impose real penalties. The judges are often landlords themselves, some say, and see only the landlord's side. Others say the landlords make big contributions to the political clubs that elect judges. Again, the relative political impotence of the poor is their housing handicap.

* Peter S. McGhee, "From Pasture to Squalor," *Nation*, March 23, 1964, p. 295.

One judge came to the aid of tenants. When thirteen tenants, haled to court by their landlords, brought five dead rats to court, hidden under coats, the rent strike lid was lifted. Tenants were permitted to give rents to the court until repairs were made and the rats evicted. A second judge ruled that tenants could keep their own rents until repairs were made.

A flurry of tenant self-help activity followed. East Harlem's first tenement cooperative was soon set up. Tenants in one building voted to continue paying full rent—to themselves—even though the city had reduced rents. The money went into a fund to pay the janitor and buy coal. The old janitor was discharged and a new one hired by the tenants. There was some emotional debate about what should be done with six rent-delinquent tenants, and eviction was threatened.

It was midwinter, and people were cold. They wanted action. Groups everywhere began to organize. The East Harlem CORE chapter, working in the Triangle, was one of the first groups. "Landlords in the ghetto are really a class of terrible people," said one twenty-year-old CORE (Congress of Racial Equality) organizer. "They're irresponsible, and that's a nice word to use."

It is hard to get to the actual owner of the buildings, organizers said. "There are so many fronts you have to go through to get to him. But I'll bet you something like 1,000 people own the 20,000 buildings in this neighborhood. They never repair. And if they do, they have someone slap some plaster on the walls that comes down in about two months. And that's after three months of fantastic pressure."*

Putting a building on rent strike and holding it there is hard work. "The court procedure is a whole lot of trouble. The

* Daniel M. Friedenberg's answer to the question "Who owns New York?" is that ownership "is an overlay of shared interests—interlocked, interwoven. These interests are the life insurance companies, the commercial banks, the powerful old and the ascendant new families, certain churches, institutions and corporations, the union finance committees, the pension funds. New York is owned by perhaps one hundred men who sit on the right committees and who say yes or no when questions of leasing and sale, of temporary con-

courts sometimes decide in your favor, and the landlord will be fined $25. And they won't follow through to find out if the repairs have been really made. The landlords have power on their side. They pay the taxes and they pay the lawyers. The landlord is in and out of the building and he scares people. Many of the Spanish people see an official paper, which is the dispossess, and they'll pay him. Or they won't communicate. Sometimes the tenants don't speak to other tenants."

CORE teams were composed of ten organizers and a captain. The team took one block, and three or four people went into each building. They got violation forms filled out and heard tenant complaints. Tenant meetings were held to voice complaints and plan action. "In case one landlord owns several buildings, you try to get them all on rent strike at once. That works much more effectively. We may hit one side of a block and get all those buildings organized. You try to get them interested in your philosophy and in the civil rights movement. It's one of our basic aims to do that."

Even more than the school boycott that preceded it, the rent strikes engaged East Harlem's citizens in the civil rights ferment. It engaged the "grass roots" and called up indigenous leaders, male as well as female. It was led by Negro and Puerto Rican residents rather than white social workers.

The rent strike's course is familiar. It began with a legal breakthrough (as in the schools) and a court decision. Then it proceeded to direct action to enforce the law and publicize its breach. Now, more and more, it is moving into political action, self-help, and outside aid programs.

---

struction money and permanent financing come up." ("The Hundred Men on the Right Committees," *Herald Tribune*, February 21, 1964.)

In New York there is a far greater concentration of land and property ownership than is generally known. Samuel J. Lefrak, for example, has more tenants in his buildings than the city itself has in public housing (half a million).

4

The houses, they should be rebuilt. No, they can't. It would take a long time. Take another project. Then take these people and move them into the project. In the projects they have more respect than they do for the old buildings. And the policeman watch the buildings. You know, there's more space. It's fire proof. And they have better supplies. From the viewpoint up on the twentieth floor you could see Central Park. A lot of things you could see. My mother don't like them because there's been too many killed. The elevators get stuck.
—A SIXTH GRADE PUERTO RICAN BOY

Urban Renewal:
The Bulldozer and the Bulldozed

The "projects" are East Harlem's landmark. The community has been "blessed" with more public-housing projects than any other in New York. The public put them there for the poor because private builders would not build low income housing. One out of three East Harlem residents is now a tenant of the government.

Almost half of all tenants in East Harlem's nine giant public developments are Negro; about one in three is Puerto Rican, and about one in five "other."

The middle-income cooperative is a new idea. In East Harlem there are two: the giant Franklin Plaza and 1270 Fifth Avenue.*

In Spanish Harlem not one housing project has a Spanish name.

---

* Though relatively few Puerto Ricans live in middle income project housing, about 18.5 per cent of apartments in forty-eight middle income projects under the city's Housing and Redevelopment Board were owned by Negroes.

TABLE I. East Harlem Public Housing Developments (Per Cent)

Project	Sponsorship	Negroes	Puerto Ricans	Whites
Wagner	federal	34	41	25
East River	federal	43	34	29
Washington	federal	40	49	11
Lexington	city	55	25	20
Taft	city	57	34	6
Johnson	state	75	25	—
Jefferson	federal	33	33	33
Carver	state	43	34	29
Wilson	state	45	28	25
MEDIAN		47	34	19

In fact, not a single major institution in East Harlem bears a Spanish name; not even the great name of Luis Muñoz is there. Only two projects are named after Negroes: George Washington Carver and James Weldon Johnson.

The low income projects greatly reduced East Harlem's white "other" population.*

On the whole the projects, with one in five white tenants, have been fairly well integrated, far better than in private housing.

Minors in public housing outnumber adults.† Swollen and congested youth populations in the slum tend to give the "youth culture" more power than the adult culture, and often puts it out of the reach of adult authority. Middle income housing tends to reduce the proportions of the youth group in the slum. The only project in East Harlem where adults outnumber minors is the Lexington Houses, a small project that has a higher family income than any other project. There, adults outnumber minors two to one.

Overwhelmingly, project families are self-supporting. Only 14 per cent are on public welfare, and only 2.3 per cent are

---

* Whites were 34 per cent of site tenants before Washington Houses (public housing) were put up, and 8 per cent after; 81 per cent of the Wagner Houses site and 21 per cent after; 64 per cent of the Jefferson Houses site and 28 per cent after. In no cases did the proportion of whites increase when public housing came in.

† In seven projects there were some 20,000 minors and 17,000 adults.

considered "problem families." The projects give the transient slum neighborhood both stability and continuity. Turnover in the projects, including transfer to other projects, has been very low, about 5 per cent a year. The projects are such a good buy that tenants seldom leave by choice. They are such a good buy that each year there are 85,000 applicants for the 6,000 project vacancies in the city.

Still, some people call East Harlem a raped community. The accused rapist is not the slum landlord but the public bulldozer.

The most heated debate in East Harlem now is over urban renewal, what should be renewed and how. Everyone favors renewal, more or less. The dispute is over who is going to make the decisions about renewal. The city says it has the ultimate power of decision-making. Some "community leaders" say that the community should either make the decisions or approve all decisions that are made. The average citizen is not much involved: He doesn't like his slum housing at all, but he doesn't want simply to be chased out to perhaps worse housing while the city tears down his slum.

The loudest complaints about East Harlem's giant projects have been: too much upheaval too fast, failure to relocate the bulldozed into decent housing, poor housing design, too many rules, failure to consult the community.

Some feel the bulldozer tore down diversity and put up a high-rise ghetto. Hundreds of small stores and businessmen were displaced. Handsome and sturdy old brownstones, clubs, and meeting places were torn up along with the tenements. Italians and other whites and what there was of the middle class were displaced and scattered.

There was so much bulldozing, and it was done so fast. "They simply need a breather," some city officials say about the East Harlem critics of renewal. Like a patient undergoing a decade of painful surgery, East Harlem needs to pause a bit, they said, recover its health, and let the incisions mend.

Social workers who welcomed the bulldozer expected miracles and were disillusioned to find that new housing did not end
all social and personal ills on the spot. So they turned on what
were essentially their own creations. One social worker critic
of bulldozing said: "In the late forties and fifties, we thought
that soon our settlement houses could close their doors. Public
housing would solve everyone's problems and redemption would
be upon us. The settlements had been out in front in the fight
for good housing and slum clearance. Now, after ten years of
relocation and rebuilding, we pulled our heads out of the sand
of overwork and looked around us. Our neighbors didn't seem
to be accepting all this beneficence with the right spirit of grace.
They were looking to us for help, and we were longing for the
good old days. For *then* we could blame everything on bad
housing."

The Triangle is being studied for renewal, but "we don't
want the whole area torn out," said one CORE organizer.
"Where are these people going to go? We have mothers without
husbands, families that cannot get into public housing." Some of
the CORE youths feel that the bulldozer should knock down
everything. "The whole area needs to come down," said one
youth. "Everybody north of Ninety-sixty Street will say the
same. You need a brand-new place. Our chapter had a plan to
tear down Harlem and have the youth of Harlem build it up.
This way you would have jobs and you would rebuild the community." However feasible, the idea is a perfect response to
East Harlem's job and housing needs. Relocation could start by
building on vacant land (perhaps over the Park Avenue tracks
as Percival Goodman suggests), then moving people in as the
bulldozer tears down the slums.

The view of some of East Harlem's leaders about the projects
was well stated in the Town Meeting report of June 1960,
following a citizen study of the community. Before the advent
of public housing, it said, "East Harlem was a community that
had much that was healthy and good and important. There

were newcomers and oldtimers, storekeepers, churches, civic and fraternal organizations and a great variety of life flowing in and out of the buildings." There were too many slums however and the "greatest and first need was for low-income housing. Government moved in to meet this need. The method used might be termed 'bull-dozing,' that is, the haphazard selection of block after block to be torn down resulting in the hurried relocation of thousands of families, the elimination of small businessmen, and the frantic struggle by former residents to secure an apartment in the new project."

The projects "brought islands of hope to many people in our community, scores of new parks and playgrounds, and many community centers which provide our residents with the opportunity to experiment in civic leadership. Many tenant associations are forming, and a new spirit of concern and participation in community life is coming forward."

Criticisms were: "Because of the lack of centralized planning, and the failure to take the total needs of our community into account, there have been some unfortunate aftereffects. Our projects were all low-income projects. Families who earned more than a specified amount couldn't apply; families who moved in and whose income began to rise had to move out . . . no one could predict the location of the next housing project. Finally, the new projects made no provision for the people who did not fall into the 'low income' category. . . . But we are pleased to see that the city administration is experimenting with alternatives to bull-dozing. The new emphasis on neighborhood conservation is indeed welcomed by us as a community. . . ."

Because the settlements were less than happy with the new projects, Ellen Lurie, a whirlwind volunteer organizer, made a study in the mid-1950s of Washington Houses, a new low income project. About a third of the 637 families were interviewed. Average rent, including utilities, was low, $44.11. About 13 per cent of families were on welfare.

Before the project, 1,420 *unrelated* individuals lived on the site. There were *none* in the project; tenants were all families. In the old neighborhood 36 per cent of housing units had no private bath and 32 per cent no running water. In the projects all units had both baths and running water. The project lowered density from 444 persons per acre to 273. It raised the percentage of Negroes from 42 per cent to 88 per cent. It lowered the age of residents. Before the project, 12 per cent of residents were younger than five, 27 per cent after. In the project only 15 per cent of women had jobs, compared with 33 per cent in the old neighborhood.

About half of the families had no friends in the project. Many did not want friends and preferred anonymity. Out of more than 200 families, 47 were active church members, 26 belonged to tenant groups, 16 to unions, 12 to social clubs, 4 to political clubs. In these cases, they were more than nominal members. About a third of the families had no father. More than 15 per cent of the families suffered mental or physical disabilities.

Interviewers noted:

—On annual inspection, one family was found with bare cupboard, practically no furniture, and virtually starving children.

—One man, a veteran who suffered from nervous fits since the war, was almost completely cured after leaving his one-room basement and coming here to a lovely four-room apartment with his wife and two children.

—Mrs. B lived with her husband at a Central Park apartment for twenty-two years. Childless, she kept on working at a bakery-restaurant around the corner. Now both her apartment and the bakery have been torn down. Although she has lived in Washington Houses for more than a year, she still has her pictures and mirrors on the floor waiting to be hung. The living room looks as though she moved in yesterday—or planned to move away tomorrow. She thinks the project is too cold and public a place. Her old building was homey and friendly and private. She was terribly frightened once in an elevator when a Puerto Rican man smiled at her. She cried for a long time during the interview. Although it was mid-afternoon, she was still in night clothes, lying on the sofa. She had no friends here, but still goes back to the site to visit her friends in buildings not yet vacated.

—Many react by simply ignoring their new home, using it only as a place to sleep, continuing to go back to the old neighborhood for friends, for church, and even for shopping.

—The white families were generally a fairly unhappy lot to interview. Three of the white women dissolved into tears during the conversations. Negative reactions ranged from disappointment in finding the neighborhood changed from the way they remembered it to outraged resentment and anger at the world for allowing them to live in such a community. Secretly, they often seem ashamed of themselves for not being able to do better, and they spend much time discussing all the places where they would prefer to be. Many of them simply feel uncomfortable, lost because they can't find any neighbors they consider their equals, or any children they would like to see play with their own.

—Mrs. Walker's apartment was pitch black at 3:00 in the afternoon, with all the windows drawn and the television playing. Mrs. Walker has two children and is expecting a third. Although her baby is due in a month, she hasn't yet seen a doctor. She told how she had eaten rat poison when she was an infant and was blinded for some time. She still wears extremely thick glasses and has vision in one eye only. However, the years of treatment for her eyes at Bellevue frightened her away from doctors, and although she has tuberculosis, the doctors can't catch her for an X-ray. She thinks this is very amusing. Her husband was wounded in the legs in the Navy and doesn't work. During the entire long interview, she kept the two children on the floor, with the one-year-old naked on a potty. "I've almost got her broke," she kept saying, hitting the child every time she tried to get off.

The study was suggestive rather than conclusive. It suggested that projects are not a panacea, that tenants needed far more attention than they were getting, and a better chance to belong and meet neighbors. It did not suggest that tenants were happier in the old slums than in their new homes. Out of this study came the East Harlem Project (a grass roots self-help project that will be discussed later) and its efforts to organize project tenants.

"Ever since 1949, when the national Housing Act was passed," said Lewis Mumford, commenting on Jane Jacobs' writings, "cities of this country have been assaulted by a series of vast federally aided building operations. These large-scale operations have brought only small-scale benefits to our city. The people who gain by the government's handouts are not the displaced slum dwellers but the new investors and occupants. . . . There is nothing wrong with these buildings except that, humanly speaking, they stink. Sanitary steam-heated apartments, she [Jane Jacobs] observed, are no substitute for warmhearted neighbors, even if they live in verminous cold-water flats."* The poor don't seem to agree. They clearly prefer sanitation and steam heat to warmhearted neighbors, though they would like to have both, plus many other things the projects do not offer. For many "professionals," writers, social workers, architects, the city and its projects are the villains. For the poor the villain is more often the slumlord. If the poor were able to mark the city and the slumlord, the city might get a C plus and the latter might fail or be thrown out of school.

The public's big failure was that it seldom asked the social workers or the people about anything. It simply brought in the bulldozer and tore down the slums (and everything else good and bad that got in the way). So far as the poor were concerned, the renewer often seemed like a cowboy rounding up his herd, moving it from one bad grazing land to another. The city, of course, behaved much better than the private builders who have

* Lewis Mumford, "The Sky Line," *New Yorker*, December 1, 1962.

torn up New York. Private builders neither consulted, warned, nor relocated. The dispossessed had no appeal.

"Relocation is the most emotionally charged part of renewal," said Relocation Commissioner Herman Badillo. The critics demand that tenants be relocated in better housing, that new projects be built on vacant sites, that good housing and commerce be preserved. They demand better project design and diversity of people and buildings. They want to keep street life. Above all, they want the community to be closer in on decision-making.

Unlike many slums East Harlem (and Central Harlem even more so) contains many sound and beautiful old buildings. They were put there by the rich and well-to-do. They were not built to be slums, as were the tenements, and they are not to this day. They need renovation, not removal. The city has tried to do this, but the renovation is expensive and puts rentals out of reach of the poor.

East Harlem had unplanned bulldozing for a decade, starting in 1945. After that, urban renewal, community renewal, and conservation—more humane programs—have replaced the heavy edge of the bulldozer.* Much more public money will be spent

---

* The first federal low income housing law was enacted in 1937 by the New Deal. An affirmation came in the Housing Act of 1949. The urban renewal concept was added in 1954, introducing rehabilitation of older housing, along with demolition and construction.

In ten years of slum clearance under the federal Title 1, New York City put up 18,000 units, *seven times the number of any other city,* to replace old tenements. Slums spread as fast as the new buildings go up.

More federal funds for public housing are needed. The Federation of Settlements comments: "New York City alone could well use the 35,000 units of public housing authorized by Congress." Low rent public housing should comprise 10 per cent of the annual housing production—or more than 200,000 units each year, the federation has said (*A New Look at Public Housing*, New York; National Federation of Settlements and Neighborhood Centers).

It is estimated that 200,000 more low income apartments are needed in New York City. Since 1945, 111,000 have been built; 43,000 tenements of the kind outlawed in 1901 still stand, with more than 400,000 tenants; 49,000 new-law tenements, most in deplorable condition, still stand.

In 1963 more new housing was built in New York City than in thirty-four years. But only 3,000 low rent public housing units were built, compared with 6,800 in 1962.

on housing in East Harlem. The use of this money may decide the community's fate. That is why the issue burns so hot.

Much of the criticism of renewal in East Harlem and other places has come from the clergy and from professionals, who understandably do not want their churches and offices torn down and their congregations and clientele dispersed by renewal. Their own best interests may or may not, however, be identical to the best interests of East Harlem's citizens.

A leading Protestant minister said, "Despite enormous public investments and efforts of social agencies, East Harlem remains essentially a slum. Why? Because the people do not have power. The community has suffered as much as it has been helped. . . . It has suffered especially from public investment." This is a strong statement, an overstatement. East Harlem has suffered in some ways from public investment. Its life has been, to some extent, sterilized by project living; and old neighborhood bonds have been broken, for good or evil. But the sickness of East Harlem comes much less from public investment than from private and, to a less extent, public neglect.

The city is reluctant to give up authority on renewal to the community. Renewers say that the city must lead and the community advise, not the reverse. The city's renewal director said that some critics think the local community is the "vessel of all truth and wisdom." This leads to "complete stultification of progress, planned anarchy where nothing is accomplished." Of the two communities—local and general (city)—the general community, he said, should have authority to make the final decisions.

Ellen Lurie left her work in East Harlem because she was not sure that the city should be fought so hard on renewal. Many East Harlem leaders who have no professional "stake" in preserving the community as is feel that the community's biggest need is to tear down the slums, fast, and put up decent housing.

Protests from the bulldozed have grown. Saul Alinsky's TWO (Temporary Woodlawn Organization, a mobilization project in Chicago's South Side) has opposed renewal initiated by the University of Chicago. In other projects also he has successfully organized communities against urban renewal. In these efforts he has been supported and sponsored mainly by the clergy and local businessmen who would be forced by renewal to forfeit large investments in church buildings and other properties, not to mention members and customers. Strong supporters of renewal, on the other hand, have been banks, "downtown" business, and politicians who want to make a record.

Protest against renewal has not yet yielded much return. Once a renewal plan is made, approved, and launched, it is usually too late for protest. The poor have been impotent to fight renewal, except with such aid as given by groups like TWO. Rarely does renewal dare intrude into an articulate middle class community. It tried in New York's Greenwich Village and was badly beaten. Negroes and other poor have nowhere had comparable success.

PERSPECTIVE

Renewal, because it causes change as nothing else short of revolution, is East Harlem's most vital and hotly contested issue, by professionals at least. It is much less vital an issue than jobs and employment, which would permit East Harlem tenants to move out on their own into better housing. But public money is not available for jobs. It is available for renewal and hence the debate.

That many tenements in East Harlem should come down, and quickly, is apparent to anyone who looks inside them or talks to their tenants. Renewal is needed—informed renewal. While the rent strikes brought the slums to public attention, improved some buildings, and helped organize some slum tenants, the rent strike is not, cannot be, the answer to East Harlem's housing problem. It cannot tear down the tenements that are beyond feasible repair and put up decent integrated housing. This is the only solution that has real meaning in East Harlem. Demolition and rebuilding, of course, should be done in consultation with the community, and every effort should be made to move site tenants, as a neighborhood unit, into new buildings before the old buildings are demolished. If units could be put up on vacant or commercial land, they could house those whose homes are marked for demolition. This way site tenants would not be scattered and neighboring patterns destroyed, and new slums would not be created in other areas. All projects should of course be integrated racially and economically in so far as possible.

Professionals and tenants together should, instead of waiting on the city, make their own applications for federal money to engage in self-help, rehabilitation, and cooperative ownership projects.

If anything, the rent strikes have lured back the bulldozer. The New York City Planning Commission chairman announced not long after the heat of the strikes had passed that he would bring back the bulldozer, which had been inactive during the 1960s, and move out into the worst slums. "We've been trying to do urban renewal without taking down any buildings, moving any people or hurting anybody. Now we're going again into the areas that have to be bulldozed."

How grand a plan is desired? Percival Goodman, architect brother of writer Paul Goodman, drew up a dramatic new plan for East Harlem. It included much street removal and total rebuilding. While designs for slums should take some moon shots, nobody wants to go this far yet. The total lack of imaginative planning and design in East Harlem is appalling. That the Puerto Ricans, Negroes, and Italians can somehow make this an interesting, and in some absurd way even an attractive, community is a great tribute to their own personal resources. The physical part of the community, both old and new, seems engaged in a mortal combat with its citizens to prevent the emergence of the esthetic, the imaginative, the pleasant.

5

What makes me proud of being myself is—I don't know. Like in the school you find you're going into the top smart class. That for me makes me proud. I haven't felt proud in a long time.
—ELEVEN-YEAR-OLD NEGRO BOY

Schools: Broken Ladder to Success

School administrators have been under fire in East Harlem and elsewhere. In New York's Lower East Side, school principals locked horns with the area's Mobilization for Youth project; charges and demands for resignation were made on both sides. The principals claimed they were being harassed by the parents.

Such parent arousal is new to these schools. Formerly, the word of the school authorities was gospel. The new vocal chords that parents in slum schools are exercising are hard to manage. The new voice comes out loudly at first, louder than intended, as the bottled up complaints burst forth. Then parents learn to speak in normal tones. In the meantime schoolmen will probably continue to take a verbal beating and perhaps worse. Many have asked for it; some have not.

Parents blame the school for the child's failure to achieve. The

47

school blames the parents, directly or by implication. In some cases the blame is harsh: "They [the poor] are animals. They don't care about their children. How can *we* be expected to do anything?" More often the "blame" takes the form of pity rather than accusation: "They are so poor and deprived and apathetic that they can't do anything. The families are broken, the children have no fathers. What can the school do?"

Both pity and accusation have the same effect: the abandonment of hope and responsibility for achievement and change. While some schoolmen have now turned from low IQ scores to conditions and "deprivation" in the home as explanations of failure, few have turned to the school for explanations. Those asking for change have favored a "different" program of instruction for the poor. A good idea, but what it has often meant in practice is "easy learning" or detours around mastery of academic skills.

A composition written by a sixth grade Puerto Rican boy in East Harlem, and reproduced exactly as written, reveals the size of the problem:

"I would like to have good teachers because some teachers like to hit the children so the children don't come to school because of that. Some of the classmates like to pick on the children that don't like to fight so the classmates pick on them. Some school don' give good lunch and some of the window are broken. The chairs aren't good the desk are bombing and you can't write on it and some of the hallway are written with chalk or crayon. Some teachers don't teach us in every subjects. So the children don't learn alot. So the teachers leave them leave back."

> *We, the Puerto Rican people, in our way of life, do not practice separation of race either by law, by custom, by tradition or by desire. Notwithstanding this and suspectedly because of this, in the nomenclature of race relations on the Continent, we are designated neither White nor Negro, but a special group denominated Puerto Ricans.*

This objectivity, aggravated by our distinctiveness of culture has made us the victims of the same type of discrimination and social persecution that is visited upon the Negro group of this Country. The result has been to make us more conscious of the justice and righteousness of the cause of the Negro in America today. We therefore, feel impelled to identify ourselves with the Negro's struggle and lend him our support, while at the same time conserving our own cultural integrity and our way of life.

We, therefore, launch ourselves into the arena of today's struggles for a full and complete education alongside the Negro with the full knowledge that by so doing we are advancing our own cause.

–PREAMBLE TO THE "DRAFT RESOLUTION ON THE EDUCATION OF THE PUERTO RICAN CHILD IN NEW YORK CITY," ISSUED BY THE NATIONAL ASSOCIATION FOR PUERTO RICAN CIVIL RIGHTS, FEBRUARY 6, 1964.

East Harlem schools are segregated schools in the sense that, in all but four schools, 90 per cent of the students are Negro and Puerto Rican. They are not segregated in the sense that Central Harlem's schools are segregated. The Puerto Ricans, a large percentage of them light skinned, make the difference. East Harlem's schools do not look segregated. Indeed, if the "nomenclature of race relations" designated Puerto Ricans as white, the schools in East Harlem would be fully integrated.

The Puerto Ricans' feelings about segregated schools are very different from the Negroes'. They do not have the history and the sense of exclusion that Negroes have, and, because many of them are in fact white, they have much less trouble "integrating."

When the first citywide school integration boycott in New York came along, the citizens' school committee of East Harlem hesitated. Puerto Ricans were not strong for protest or integration, the feelings of whites were mixed, and strong Negro sentiment was not forthcoming for various reasons. After lengthy debate, led mainly by whites on both sides, the school committee finally supported the boycott. On the day of the boycott, its support was, like Central Harlem's, more than 90 per cent effective.

Whatever else it did, the boycott sparked parent and community interest in East Harlem. Parents and youths poured into the preboycott rally, and the older hands who had been begging parents to attend meetings asked, "Where did they all come from?" They came to protest. They had grievances, and they came to air them. For many of these parents it was the first time at a school meeting. Few Negro or Puerto Rican men attended, but the women came, and a number of white men.

School integration achieved by busing, a method championed in New York mainly by middle class Negroes in the ghetto, has had less appeal in East Harlem than in other places. Puerto Ricans have held back from the integration and civil rights struggle, and many whites in East Harlem school groups feared that busing would remove the active parents from the schools. These whites seem to have one object: to build East Harlem into a real community. Both urban renewal and bused integration run contrary to their goal when they threaten to disrupt the community and remove the more "participating" citizens.

When East Harlem turned out for the integration boycott it was the first time in the community's history, or the city's, that Puerto Ricans joined with Negroes in protest and pursuit of a common goal.

Even the militant CORE youths, committed to organizing and building in the neighborhood, were lukewarm to busing anyone out of the community. They wanted to upgrade the neighborhood schools and tended to read citizen sentiment as also indifferent to bused integration. One Negro organizer said: "The people in the community are not interested in integration. They just want better schools and better teaching for their kids. In Central and West Harlem there are many people who have a slightly better income level, slightly better earning capacity, and are more articulate than people in East Harlem and want integration."

And a white organizer joined in: "The integration issue is irrelevant if you're trying to beat the rats off your children at night. We're not up to that point yet. You have to be above the survival level—I shouldn't speak not being black—you haven't got much energy left. Not only that, integration is a horrible experience for people. If your children are limited in the education they get, you really put them through a terrible experience by sending them elsewhere."

Still, East Harlem went all out for New York's first integration boycott . . . but not for the second.

A powerful argument for school integration is found in the transfer of eighty-three students from East Harlem to white, middle class Yorkville.

"We found children who improved in many ways following transfer," a report said.* "In one, or two, just a handful of cases, there was little noticeable change, but in the majority of cases the children showed dramatic improvement in their school work, in their attendance and, generally they showed renewed vigor and interest in school."

After parent protest, these East Harlem children had been bused to white schools to relieve overcrowding and promote integration. Only 7 per cent of eligible children in one school and 2 per cent in the other signed up to transfer. Of these, fifty-eight were Negroes, twenty-two were Puerto Ricans, and three were Chinese.

Both the parents and children were far from being the most destitute in these schools. Of the 83 who transferred, 34 were reading on or above grade level. Most parents set high educational goals for their children. Sixty-seven parents planned that their children complete high school; 39 that they attend college; and another 14 favored college if other conditions were met. Only 16 had not attended parent meetings in school. Fifty of the parents had attended high school, 21 were high school

* *Releasing Human Potential*, prepared by the East Harlem Project and the New York City Commission on Human Rights, 1961.

graduates, and 4 had some college. Fifty-two of the children had fathers at home: Forty-one did manual labor, 11 had professional or white collar jobs. Only 10 mothers were employed full time.

What happened to student conduct at the integrated school? There were 13 changes reported, all improvements. As for interest in school, 47 showed an increase, one a decrease. There were 13 changes in attendance records, all improvements. There were 52 changes of "work habits"; 51 were improvements and one was a decline. Only 5 parents said they were disappointed with the transfer; 11 were "pretty well satisfied"; and 55 said that they were "well satisfied."

Some people complained that the most interested parent leadership "had bused their children out and were lost to East Harlem's schools." For this reason they opposed further bused integration.

It appears much easier to integrate schools that are not coeducational. In 1959 East Harlem's Benjamin Franklin High School was all boys. It was 29 per cent Negro, 28 per cent Puerto Rican, and 43 per cent "other," i.e. white. When it became coeducational, in 1960, the "others" dropped from 43 per cent to 20 per cent. Catholic schools that are sexually segregated are, for this reason, easier to integrate racially.

Increasingly, both whites and Negroes are leaving the public school integration crisis and transferring to Catholic parochial schools. Both go to escape mounting Negro enrollment in public schools. Before World War II, one in twelve students in the United States was enrolled in Roman Catholic schools; now the ratio is one in eight. Catholic school enrollment between 1945 and 1962 increased 129 per cent (to 5.5 million students), while public school enrollment grew only 69 per cent (to 38.8 million students). The integration conflict seems to be swelling parochial schools.

Some Catholic schools in East Harlem provide a common meeting place where racially mixed youth groups heve relatively familiar contact. There are few such places in East Harlem.

The Catholic schools are strictly disciplined, and parents are virtually required to attend school meetings. East Harlem's St. Cecilia's Church bulletin, in a message to parents, said, "After a short business meeting the parents will meet the teachers and receive their report cards." Report cards are one insurance that parents will come. The Catholic school is better able to handle integration than the public school for at least three reasons; segregation of the sexes in many Catholic schools, the natural and sometimes arbitrary controls of ethnic mixture, and centralized church authority.

In New York about half of all Negro and Puerto Rican children go to public schools that are at least 10 per cent "other" (white). It is not known what proportion of these integrated minority children are Negro. In New York the biggest integration hurdle is the primary school. Secondary school students can travel on their own to integrated schools. Small children cannot, and their parents (both Negro and white) are often reluctant to have them bused outside the neighborhood. A state education department report proposed educational parks as a long-range integration solution and, for the short term, an integrated "middle school," starting in the fifth grade (5 through 8), to which children would be bused if necessary. The purpose of these proposals is to make integration possible by drawing students from a larger and more heterogeneous area. The feasibility of these parks is unknown since few people have much experience with them.

THE QUALITY ISSUES

> *We're asking for a new school. It will be a ghetto school, but we can improve the educational level and move them downtown. For four years they say, "Well, you'll have your school this year." Then they say, "We can't fit it into the city budget."*

> *They said they had no money for repairs. Then after three*
> *boycotts, they sent some men around to build a garbage bin*
> *and they also built some partitions around the toilets. They*
> think *that way! You bug them and they put up a board around*
> *the toilet which is in the lunchroom.*
>
> —AN EIGHTEEN-YEAR-OLD CORE ORGANIZER

Education is said to be a ladder for the poor to climb up, but
in East Harlem it is rickety and many steps are missing. Of the
sixteen elementary schools in East Harlem, twelve have over-
capacity enrollment. Four out of five junior high schools are
overcrowded.* The result is a short school day for students who
should have a long one.

Educators stress nursery and early childhood education. Yet
only a few of East Harlem's schools had a full five-hour *first
grade*. About one out of three or four children, it is estimated,
enter first grade without kindergarten. Space for kindergarten
classes has been in short supply, and the schools have seldom
recruited among parents for enrollment. Often there has been
a long waiting list for kindergarten. In New York children who
have gone to kindergarten are usually put automatically in top
"ability groups" in first grade, where they tend to stay through-
out school.

New schools in East Harlem came slowly and never kept up
with demands made by new housing projects and population.
Schools should be included in the ground floors of new projects
in order to keep pace with population growth and integrate the
school into the community.

"Tear down the armory, and put up a school" was the slogan
of an East Harlem mass demonstration. The site demanded was
an "integrated" one within white territory to the south. The
armory has been used, among other things, as a polo ground by
wealthy East Siders and as a police stable. Citizen demands have
persuaded the board to earmark funds for a school on the site.

---

* The total overload is 2,700 in the elementary schools and 440 in the junior
highs as of the end of 1963.

One school that would send pupils to the proposed new school, had three different principals in five years and a 90 per cent turnover of teachers. While the average teacher-turnover in New York City as a whole has been 10 per cent, the turnover in East Harlem has been 20 to 25 per cent.

In one recent year, 57 per cent of East Harlem's school teachers had permanent licenses, 25 per cent were substitutes, 18 per cent had probationary licenses. In the junior highs, 44 per cent had permanent licenses and 43 per cent were substitutes. Many licensed teachers in junior highs taught subjects they were not licensed to teach. Many with only elementary licenses were teaching in junior highs.*

Reading and IQ scores of East Harlem children decline with age. In the third grade, students in one district scored 2.8 on a reading test compared with the city average of 3.5. By the eighth grade, the East Harlem students were two full years below grade level.

By the eighth grade their IQ score was 83.2, compared with 103.4 for the city. In the third grade it had been 91.2, compared with 98.8 for the city.

In the junior high schools, 12 per cent of students were reading above grade level, 8 per cent on grade level, 10 per cent one year below grade level, and 70 per cent more than one year below grade level.

As for what the children think about school, the compositions of sixth grade students, quoted exactly, describe some of their wishes and needs:

A Puerto Rican girl wrote: "I would like to be change is to have a better playground where the children could enjoy. Or perhaps a big swimming pool and around it many fountains. Or to have better clean Bathrooms and to have better teachers that could teach you all different languages. all maybe a better auditorium where many people of all over the world could come and

* Source: Bureau of Educational Research, Board of Education.

make us happy. and in the auditorium could have better comfortable seats. all maybe better hallways."

A Negro girl wrote: "I would like to have more teachers in the school where the children could have different subjects everyday. And the school need more bathrooms because they have one each bathroom on each floor, they need at least three bathrooms on each floor. And they need a bigger auditorium because this auditorium is too small for this many children that they have here."

The children are inclined to blame themselves for their failure to learn. And, on the top of their mind always is fear or concern about physical abuse. Sixth graders commented:

Suppose you were the teacher and you explained something and I said, "I wasn't listening" and you explained it again, and I wasn't listening again. You would get mad, right? Some of the kids are real bad. Some of the teachers don't know how to hit kids. You hit with a ruler. You should see the Catholic school. You talk to somebody and the sister she tell you to stand up and she takes the ruler and she hits you real hard two times on each hand.

If a person wants to learn, he will concentrate, and he wouldn't get whipped, because by whipping a person he'll just go on and do it again. Like my brother, he's real bad. He do everything in his classroom. He pull up girls' dresses. He knock down chairs. This teacher hit my brother, and he was all black and blue and he was bleeding. The teacher has no right to hit no child, they should send for his mother.

My father says if I get too much unsatisfactory, he's gonna whip me. Because if my mother waste her time getting up at 7 o'clock to wake me up, for me to do nothing, it's my fault. I admit it. I don't listen to nothing what my teacher says.

I think the teachers should treat us better, you know. We're young, we don't hardly know nothing. You know, when you tell them something, they say, "Where'd you get that strange story or something." You tell them the truth but they don't believe you or nothing. But I think it's not the teacher's fault. It's up to you. True.

TEACHERS COMMENT

Some teachers try and succeed. Others try and fail. Some don't try, at least not very hard; they give up almost before they start. One East Harlem teacher of a "medium slow" fifth grade (not a "bottom" class) was having trouble and, like many others, was at the point of throwing in the sponge:

I won't try to teach them something like social studies. They don't have the basic concepts. This is true even in reading. You can't relate to them. When they do hit a story that means something there is a dramatic difference in their comprehension. I can't say why some stories mean something and others don't. Social studies is a complete loss. Probably the only thing you can do is tell them social studies through a story, but this is not social studies. It is nothing like how laws are made or why a railroad was built in a certain place. You shouldn't call story telling social studies. . . .

This teacher had found one clue to her pupils' learning—that there was a "dramatic difference in their comprehension" when a story meant something to them, but she didn't know where to take this clue, how to find stories and social studies material that had meaning.

Another teacher of a "slow" sixth grade had found many other clues and had a different approach and attitude to her students:

By demanding correct speech at all times I have found their Spanish accents have just about disappeared by now. Their vocabularies have begun to enlarge. They must give reports orally, without a paper. They must know what they have written so well that they can remember the main ideas. At the beginning of the year I read aloud to them a great deal of the time, pointing out to them what I thought about pitch, timbre, pace, etc. Then we used a tape recorder and immediately they became self-critical, saying things like "That isn't me, is it?" and "I didn't say it that way, did I?" I didn't let them do any written work at first. After a few trips we would start to have open discussions. For a few weeks we did al-

most only talking. I tried to move them from specifics to abstracts.
. . . Then we were ready for writing. . . . During the Panama
crisis they did sequential pictures of why we went there in the first
place, how the situation grew during the years, and how things
began to deteriorate. I put the pictures up for a week. Then we discussed what the pictures meant. We had discussed the Panama
crisis so thoroughly that the students seemed to feel personal about
it by the time they sat down to divide up the topic for the
illustrations.

Though this teacher had a "bottom" group, she had suc-
ceeded, according to *her* story, in teaching the children something about social studies, even in such remote places as Panama,
and she had successfully modified their accents. Another teacher
said:

Things just don't make an impression on these children. We
haven't found the way to teach them. For some reason they don't
relate to school. The reason is that their whole culture is different.
The only way to teach them is to repeat things 25 times unless for
some reason it means something to them. They are not motivated at
home. They can't learn unless they see the specific reason for doing
something.

Another teacher feels the children have a problem of "how
to get along," and that they are learning this even up until the
third grade. Not until the fourth grade are they ready to learn
concepts. "They play too much. Discipline of themselves is a
problem—perhaps it is at the root."

One East Harlem teacher felt that "Negroes and Puerto
Ricans have incorrect perception. They probably see only vague
outlines. This would explain why they do so poorly in reading."

Many teachers complain about administrators and say that
they stand in the way of learning. One said: "Administrators
are my main problem as a teacher. They are not creative. They
think the slow child won't get things. I don't think this is fair.
For example: going to the World's Fair. Only the top three

classes will go. The children feel this and think they should live up to the expectations that they won't catch on to things."

Another teacher complains that beginning teachers are not properly briefed, that they should be told "how far down these children are." Teachers have to keep "starting over at a lower level." New teachers never get "concrete help." Administrators give teachers the wrong books; "the books are too high"; and many are "worthless." There is no communication between teachers; there should be "some way for new teachers to get rex-o-graphed materials that more experienced teachers have drawn up."

One experienced and highly rated teacher in an East Harlem school explains her monitor system for keeping order, her attitudes toward the children and the rewards they need:

> I appoint monitors at the beginning of the year. I make it clear that I will change an appointment if they are not worthy. I give awards each month based on conduct, grades, appearance, and manners. I jot down things that are outstanding for each child—good or bad. I used to give an assembly award for dressing but now the whole class dresses right so I had to give it up. They must be given recognition. For instance, right now I have left them alone for this interview. It lets them know that I trust them. I don't have monitors to take names. There is no tattletaling in my class. One way I helped build up this spirit was by taking them on trips and doing things together. They know they must act a certain way in order to do these things.

Knowledge, at its most useful, is an accumulation of wisdom and experience from the past. Teachers, custodians of this accumulated knowledge, have virtually no access to the accumulated experience of the thousands of other teachers who have been out in combat with the same problems, and who have through trial and failure worked out some successful methods. Neither the colleges of education nor the school administrators have done much to help the novice teacher who leaves her middle class cocoon to venture out into the slum school. The schools of East

Harlem are filled with these novice teachers, most of them eager but lost.

Dr. Kenneth Clark has said: "The concept of the culturally deprived child is a new stereotype, a new excuse, a new rationalization for inadequate education of minority group children. Instead of those responsible for their education being made to teach them, all sorts of alibis are provided. The only thing that will really matter is the total reorganization of the educational system in these communities.

"On the evidence available to date," he went on, "one is forced to conclude that the major reason why an increasing number of Central Harlem pupils fall below their grade levels is that substandard performance is expected of them. For this, the schools, principally its administrators, must shoulder the major responsibility, although the community must share some of the blame."*

Dr. Clark cited the data below in support of his statement:

TABLE II.   Assessment of Pupil Potentials in Central Harlem

	Principals	Assistant Principals	Teachers
1. Per cent reporting that one-fourth or less of the pupils have college level potential.	45	62	53
2. Per cent expecting one-half or fewer of their pupils to finish high school under present conditions.	32	57	46
3. Per cent expecting one-half or fewer of their pupils to finish high school under *conducive* conditions.	4	19	3
4. Per cent stating that greater learning potential in their students was a major change necessary to carrying out professional duties.	9	14	4

The Reverend Milton Galamison, leader of New York's school boycott, has contended that "in the Negro school the

* Harlem Youth Opportunities Unlimited, December 12, 1963.

child is not being taught. The basic problem we are fighting in the segregated school is one of attitude, which expresses itself in low expectations on the part of middle-class teachers whose concept of a human being is not met by these children. The most liberal teacher will say, 'If the Negro child had an equal economic, cultural and social background, he could learn as well as other children.' This if-ism results in 'not much teaching and not much learning.' "

Puerto Ricans have also reacted to the schoolman's concept of "cultural deprivation," but in a different way. The Puerto Ricans are proud of their culture. Joseph Monserrat, of the Commonwealth of Puerto Rico, asks: "Is a culture that has for four centuries been able to maintain the individual dignity, value and worth of all its members (despite differences in race and class) a deprived or disadvantaged culture when compared with one that has been striving to achieve these values and has as yet not been able to do so?"

Some of the dispute has to do with word meaning. The term "culturally deprived" suggests the negative aspects of low income culture. In some cases, as in Dr. Frank Riessman's excellent book, *The Culturally Deprived Child,** the positive aspects of this culture are stressed. This emphasis tends to boost rather than depress teacher morale and expectation.

Another version of the deprivation theme has entered the arena, put there by psychoanalysis. The school gets the child too late, the argument goes, after the early, formative years, and therefore can do very little either by integrating or improving the quality of education for the disadvantaged. While the argument has strong points, suggesting that much more attention should be given to nursery schools and the child-rearing education of parents, it also suggests what is not proven, that most Negroes and other disadvantaged adults are deficient in the affection, care, or instruction they give to infants. It also ignores the achievements of older children under ideal school

* New York: Harper & Row, 1962.

conditions and the regenerative effect on older youths and adults of civil rights activity.

What is observed in East Harlem and other slum schools is that children compare favorably in their achievement until the third and fourth grades, when they begin a relative decline. This might indicate that the critical period for the child is in these years rather than the preschool years.

Recognizing the importance of the infant years, however, it is essential that the schools reach not only the child but the mothers as well. On the assumption, true or not, that there are remediable deficiencies in parental care, the parent becomes as much an object of instruction as the child. One hypothesis that should be examined is that the children of the poor are typically put out on their own and given weighty responsibilities at an early age. The parents are burdened, and they are forced to pass on these burdens to young children. Families are often large, and children follow fast after one another. The mother of the large, impoverished family has no help with her chores and no time for the child who is no longer an infant who needs her continuous attention. The child is put on his own and given responsibilities for the care of other children. In short, the child may not be given the individual attention he needs for growth. He becomes a small adult at an age when more advantaged children are just beginning to emerge from infant dependency.

In this sense, also, "deprivation" has a double edge. The "deprived" child, because of his early adulthood, knows a great many things that the advantaged do not, too much perhaps. If the schools were able to make use of this knowledge, the "deprived" child might be at an advantage rather than a disadvantage in school.

East Harlem is split into two school districts, as it is split into two police precincts and two political (assembly) districts. The district in the north section also includes schools in Central

Harlem. The southern district includes many white, middle class schools, and Martin Mayer, one of the country's leading writers on the schools, has been chairman of its local school board, a group whose functions and powers are rather like those of parent-school groups. Both boards are said to be hard-working and close to the people. They have formed a closer link between citizen and school.

Whites tend to dominate East Harlem schools. All school principals are white and so are almost all administrators. Negroes and Puerto Ricans, in fact, have little to say officially about what goes on in East Harlem's schools. Even unofficially, as parents, they take a back seat and are usually silent. The chairman of the East Harlem Schools Committee, the main citizen group, has been a white woman whose Negro husband operates a small business. Whites usually do most of the talking and leading in the committee.

There is little true integration in parent groups. "In every school," says Mrs. Nora Bowens (a white woman who works full time on schools for the East Harlem Project), "there is one major ethnic group dominating the parent groups. There is seldom a mixture." In recent years a number of Negro and Puerto Rican leaders have come forth, and active parent groups are found in some schools.

The Schools Committee, from its inception in 1954, had spurts of energy. Until the first integration boycott, the committee was for a time at low ebb. It did not know what to do next. Its initial job had been to get new schools for East Harlem. Now many feel the committee should branch out into the troubled area of curriculum, an area that has in the past been held as the exclusive jurisdiction of schoolmen.

In East Harlem the major parent demand on curriculum is that the children improve reading and academic skills. They do not ask for dreary drills or any particular "method" of instruction. They want only improved learning. The schools are touchy about intrusions into curriculum. According to Preston

Wilcox of the East Harlem Project, the worst verbal beating he has gotten from the schools came after he asked the question at a meeting: "How can we get parents involved through curriculum?"

The Parent-Teacher Associations are criticized by many active people in East Harlem because they seldom take on any real issues. Some feel that the PTA's do only what the principal tells them to do—money-raising, cake sales, socials—and are upset when curriculum is raised.

Ellen Lurie gave much of the initial drive to the Schools Committee in the early 1950s. The first act of the committee was to petition for new schools. Ninety parents gathered and went to the Board of Estimate with proposals. "Women sat up nights working on their speeches; and Negro and Puerto Rican parents did things they never thought they could do," said Mrs. Lurie. The new schools came, but they did not automatically bring quality education. Hence, the new desire of East Harlem parents to take up curriculum and quality issues. The committee's demands for quality include: academic achievement, smaller class size, preschool programs, full five-hour first grades, remedial reading in grades 3 to 6 rather than junior high, "gifted child" classes in each school rather than in one separate school, separate classes with "positive programs" for children who are discipline problems, involvement of parents in the educational process as school aides.*

Negroes and Puerto Ricans also want the history of their

* At the time of the first school boycott, a new Puerto Rican civil rights group issued its first detailed manifesto of school demands. Its five stages of demands were:

Language: Spanish should be part of the curriculum of all elementary schools, and all teachers should have a working knowledge of Spanish. High schools: Vocational high schools as they currently exist should be abolished, along with the general course diploma. All junior highs should be integrated within a year. Reading retardation: A five-hour daily instruction period should be guaranteed; IQ tests should be abolished; changes should be made to "reflect the specialized learning problems of Puerto Ricans"; a "positive image of the Puerto Rican child and his culture must be fostered to enhance the child's motivation for learning."

Teacher training and recruitment: Since there are only 230 Puerto Rican teachers out of 40,000, intensive recruitment should be undertaken; teachers people to be taught in the schools, and not just to their own children. One young Negro CORE organizer put it this way: "I said to the history teacher, 'why are you showing me a book where there's only one paragraph about Negro history. You mean to tell me 400 years, with only one paragraph.' The teacher told me, 'Sit down. Lincoln freed the slaves and you should be glad you're in this part of the book.' Look in the index and look at page 389, one paragraph, 'Negroes.' The kids don't like this at all. Some books don't even have a paragraph. They just put down a few people like Joe Louis and Marian Anderson."

Some citizens in East Harlem are now raising questions, not only about curriculum but about the "power structure" of the schools. They want more Negro and Puerto Rican representation at high levels in the schools. As it is, of more than 1,200 top-level administrative posts in New York's school system, only about four are held by Negroes. Of some eight hundred principals, only several are Negro. Out of a nine-man city school board, only one is a Negro; and there is no Puerto Rican member—in a city where 40 per cent of public school children are Negro and Puerto Rican.

What do East Harlem's children think about school? They are seldom asked. When they are, they express little interest in what they are learning in school. The reasons they give for going to school and doing well almost always bear on future prospects, not on the rewards of learning but on other rewards

---

with Spanish accents should be accepted. Teachers should be taught greater understanding and appreciation of Negro and Puerto Rican culture, "not in sterile terms of Brotherhood but aimed at handling specific situations that destroy the dignity and morale of the Puerto Rican youngster."

Puerto Rican Representation: "Neither white dominant groups nor the Negro minority can speak for the Puerto Rican who must speak for himself." An effort should be made "to insure Puerto Rican parent participation in the process of decision-making which will influence at all levels the future of his child's education, and that such participation be received in a courteous, dignified manner." A Puerto Rican should be appointed to the next school board vacancy.

that school can offer. These remarks of sixth grade Negro and Puerto Rican boys are typical:

You go to school to get an education so when you grow up you can get a decent job, and you can have a high school diploma. You can go to a decent junior high, and then you can go to a decent high, and go to a decent college, and get a decent job. When we grow up it'll be the nuclear age, and we couldn't do the jobs our fathers do. They'll be done by machines.

If you don't go to school you'll be a nobody. You'll be a drifter all your life.

School's OK, cause when you get a job you got to count things in your mind, not on your fingers. If you don't go to school you grow up to be dumb. You won't be able to get a job.

Whenever I wake up I say, you better study, you know, to get a better education. If you study now, you could become something big. When you grow up you get a good job.

A PERSPECTIVE

Citizen unrest usually moves in an upward spiral. Among the poor it has moved in the past few years, during the peaks of the civil rights revolt, from apathy to agitation, then back to some midpoint of constructive criticism and interest.

In New York City—big, anonymous, and noisy—a person with a grievance must make a loud noise to be heard. The school boycotts and the rent strikes were that loud noise. They made the conditions of the poor at last visible and audible. But the momentum of the revolt (the agitation cycle) was slowed by many related factors and may not move on again for some time. Among these factors were: a presidential election, the civil rights and poverty bills, the summer ghetto riots that injured only Negroes but frightened everyone, the inability of Negro leaders to bargain their demands and to work in unity, the white backlash, the fatigue of Negro and white activists who wearied of danger and street demonstrations, the northern liberal retreat when the demonstrations came into the back yard, the failure of the demonstrations to produce immediate and visible results.

More than anything, the school boycotts and the demands for bused integration of *de facto* segregated students in New York brought the civil rights struggle to the door of the white middle class liberal and caused him to withdraw support from direct action and demonstration. These liberals, most of whom genuinely seek equality and integration, balked at busing and dropped away from groups like CORE, leaving their future as exclusively direct action groups in doubt.

The loudest and most racist "busing backlash" came from conservative organizations (Parents and Taxpayers) in middle class Queens. A quieter, more moderate, and sadder backlash came from sections of the Jewish community, which, more than other groups in New York, have been in contest with Negroes and Puerto Ricans over scarce facilities in the public schools. Many liberals have, furthermore, been reluctant to acknowledge the presence of unequal educational opportunities for Negroes and Puerto Ricans in the North. Their response has been: *We* did it despite discrimination, why can't *they?*

Having reached this cyclical plateau, very little mass agitation over schools can be expected in the nation's northern ghettos. This will not mean much in East Harlem since it was a reluctant partner in the boycotts in the first place, and since the Puerto Ricans keep it from being a Negro ghetto.

The integration boycott has undoubtedly had a positive effect on the schools of East Harlem. It has brought public attention and extra aid to the schools. It has clearly informed schoolmen that parents are dissatisfied with the progress of their children in school. Above all, it aroused parents and citizens in East Harlem to a new interest in the schools and showed them that they could, through their own actions, influence school policies. Schoolmen have traditionally complained that parental apathy is responsible for low achievement in slum schools. The boycott aroused many parents from this "apathy."

Insofar as East Harlem has held back from direct action in the schools, however, it seems likely to *get* less from the schools and from new aid programs than Central Harlem, Brooklyn, and other more "militant" communities. The wheel that squeaks loudest usually gets the most grease.

East Harlem schools need a lot more grease. New schools, relief from crowding, experienced teachers, preschooling, a suitable curriculum and texts, belief in the children, contact with parents, small classes—all are visible needs. Integrationists claim it is impossible to have quality education in segregated schools. This may be true, but the claim is unproved, either way. The effect of quality education on achievement in ghetto schools is unknown because it is virtually untried. Only in the last few years has much serious experimentation with teaching methods and curriculum for the disadvantaged been tried. And only now are some suitable reading materials being prepared.

Concentrated research and development in education, comparable to the R&D that in the technological and scientific worlds are regarded as essential to progress, should be supported by public and foundation funds. This educational R&D should pull together available knowledge about successful methods in educating the disadvantaged, and develop new techniques and curriculum.

It is unlikely that quality education can be brought to the slums until members of disadvantaged minorities are brought into the schools—many of them, at high and low levels, as board members and as *educational* aides either in the schools or outside them.

The schools need new ideas and new energy. One way to get them is to democratize decision-making and bring in teachers, parents, and children on decisions and planning. The organization of teachers into unions and parents into citizen groups is already beginning to bring the knowledge and wisdom of these two vital groups to bear on educational decision-making. Their participation so far has mainly taken the form of protest, brought on by their general exclusion from school decision-making.

In the money-versus-method controversy, some experts say

that only money, lots more of it, will make any difference in slum schools. On the other hand people like Martin Mayer say that money will make little or no difference, that new methods and new approaches must be found. Both money *and* methods are needed. About half as much money is being spent on New York's slum child as on the child in the better suburbs of New York. With such expenditures, the poor could, without question, be given quality education. The point is, money will not be forthcoming in such amounts, even though the nation can afford it. So the question becomes: What are the most efficient and economical ways to give top-quality education to the poor?

The complaint made by Negro leaders that the schools expect too little of Negro and Puerto Rican students is well taken. Many schoolmen do not really expect that the poor could, with proper instruction, learn as much and do as well as middle class students. This may, indeed, be the major flaw in the slum school: low expectations on the part of administrators, teachers, children, parents. This does not mean, however, that the disadvantaged can always *start* at the same place as the advantaged. The imposition of impossibly difficult texts and assignments on children inevitably leads to frustration and failure. But, with suitable methods and extra help, these children ought to be able to *end* at the same place as other children.

In East Harlem and similar communities there are, then, at least three routes to change in the schools: (1) change of attitude, motivation, expectation from failure to success; (2) new instructional and organizational methods; (3) community arousal and the power and pride it can provide to impoverished citizens.

One solution to the teacher shortage and the general shortage of educated leadership in the slum community would be to offer special housing buys to teachers in the neighborhood schools. If the housing offered were good enough, it would not only attract and hold teachers in the community, but would provide a needed link and understanding between school and community. These teachers would also provide community leadership. In East Harlem, for example, one of the most active minority group leaders and two of the most active white parents are also teachers who live and work in East Harlem. For the most part, however, teachers in slum schools are "absentee professionals" who leave the school and neighborhood promptly at three o'clock.

A very heavy burden has been put on slum schools. It is put there because there are so few other services and institutions in the slum community. So the school must tend to the intellectual, emotional, recreational, organizational, etc., needs of children and adults in the community—or at least it is asked to try. Other groups and agencies should be brought in to help carry this heavy weight. In particular, a massive volunteer program of youths and adults, recruited from the community, universities, women's clubs, church groups, etc., should be drawn in to help with tutorials, trips, and other instructional needs.

Though the problems of East Harlem's schools are glaringly visible, it should be said that in many schools the impression is one of health, not sickness. Teachers can be found in every school who are creative and effective and who like and respect the children. Most of East Harlem's children seem to like school, and most are well treated. Moreover, most of the children appear well dressed, clean, happy, and healthy. It is striking to the stranger who may be expecting tattered urchins or a scene from *Oliver Twist* or *The Blackboard Jungle*. This is perhaps the neglected part of the story. The better known and more tragic part is that so much is wrong; so much is needed and so little received.

It is the same as in the neighborhood. Health and disease live alongside each other—great strength and serious weakness. We tend to pick on the soft spots, the weaknesses, because they need attention. At the same time the strengths need to be seen, credited, and built upon.

6

Religious Tranquilizers and Agitators

Like other poor, many people of East Harlem, seeking comfort, rest and solace, turn to the church. Others turn to the church for social action.

Three major and distinct church groups exist in East Harlem: Roman Catholic, white middle class Protestant, and evangelical Negro and Puerto Rican. Those most concerned with social revival in East Harlem, by far, are the middle class Protestants. The spiritual revivalists are the evangelicals. Catholics are the most numerous and tread an uneasy course between the interests of their Italian and Puerto Rican members.

The white Protestant community-wide social action program is unique. Church services are somewhere midway between the two other groups. Some say they are neither fish nor fowl: They do not have the spectacle and authority of the Catholics, nor the warmth, emotionalism, and simplicity of the evangelicals. With few exceptions their places of worship are unadorned churches rather than storefronts.

Services are often a strange blend of the "high" and "low" church. One Protestant service began with the solemn and formal hymn "Come, O Come, Emmanuel" sung by the choir (all Negro female) and sounding almost like a Catholic chant: "Bid envy, strife and quarrels cease; fill the whole world with heaven's peace." Services closed with the singing of the lively Negro spiritual: "O rise! shine! for thy light is a-comin'; My Lord says he's comin' by 'n by. This is the time for Joy and Mirth, My Lord says he's comin' by 'n by . . ."

Three ministers officiated: a white woman, a Negro man, and a Puerto Rican man. Church services for these ministers must be a considerable strain. There is so much variety, improvisation, face-to-face contact with the congregation, combined with rituals that must be performed with the same precision as the Catholic mass. The three ministers showed a visible nervousness, stage fright. In contrast, Catholic mass is far more fixed; and the mark of Protestantism—individualism—is virtually absent. Responses from the congregation in the mass are few, most are group responses, and all are patterned, leaving no room for individual improvisation. Perhaps this is the power of the mass— and the Catholic church. The individual is enveloped by the group and the church. He knows the group's secrets—when to stand, when to sit, when to pray—and he is certain that the future will be like the past. The authority of the universe is providing for him. He belongs and is not alone. He does not have to stand up by himself and perform. His most individual act may be walking down the aisle to receive communion, but even this is patterned, quite passive, and done with a group. The new Catholic mass is closer to the people and gives more opportunity for lay participation, though not for individual improvisation.

In the "typical" Protestant East Harlem service, the minister's first act was to descend from the altar and ask for individual spoken responses from the congregation. Individuals stood or sat and announced meetings of school committees, commented on the tragic fire in the neighborhood, urged people to take part in the schools, asked for prayers for relatives or friends. At the end of the service, the members of the congregation were asked to shake hands with the people around them, an act requiring unusual individual initiative.

This church, anxious to reach Puerto Ricans, had dual bible readings and sermons in English and Spanish, a heavy burden for a congregation with only a few Puerto Ricans. The sermon was far more spiritual than social.

Entering a Catholic church several blocks down the street was rather like changing from sackcloth to silk. The church is large and splendid, in the manner of the most elegant churches of Italy, embossed everywhere with gold, and containing dozens of statues, ornate decorations, plaques in honor of church members, stained glass windows. White lilies and bouquets of flowers surrounded the altar. The sermon asserted that the Virgin Mary had never committed the original sin of sex. Other than the sex taboo, nothing temporal was mentioned. The mass was fairly well attended, mainly by older Italian women, and about a dozen Negroes could be seen in a congregation of roughly 250. The church has six masses on Sunday, including an 11 o'clock mass where the sermon is in Spanish.

A leaflet warned people "to conduct yourselves at these Christmas parties according to Christian principles of morality and decency" because of the holy season. It announced that "the drawing of the December booster club took place last Wednesday night. We had 13 winners. You will receive the list of all the winners with today's bulletin after Mass. The numbers assigned to our parish are C 9001–C 10200."

The Pentecostal Church specializes in togetherness, friendliness, activity, excitation, warmth—special low income Puerto Rican and Negro qualities. While the middle class Protestant church treats strangers with polite cordiality, the Pentecostal

Church draws the stranger in and treats him as part of the snug family. The storefront church, resembling the Puerto Rican living room, may have green walls, bright colors, naked light bulbs, and baby carriages crowded in the aisles. Spirited Spanish hymns will be sung, accompanied by instruments such as the tambourine and much group hand-clapping. No organs. No solemn hymns. The characteristic low income physical restlessness and demonstrativeness will be built into the service. The exchange between minister and congregation often resembles a Simon-says exercise: The minister asks for a show of hands; he asks for "amens," or a clap of hands, or that individuals rise. The congregation responds. It is never without something to do. In the far-out evangelical sects, movement is even more extreme, sometimes violent. The minister is close to the people and usually untrained in formal theology. He is more likely to be a natural leader than is the ordained clergyman, who may rate high in scriptural interpretations but low in charisma. He is otherworldly, often involved in group social welfare but remote from community social action. It is the larger society's loss that such flashes of charisma are spent so exclusively on spiritual rather than social revival.

In part because of its leaders, the Pentecostal Church is more a church for men than the Catholic or traditional Protestant churches. The male is dominant. Among Puerto Ricans, the family is usually led into the church by the male, and may just as quickly be led out. Pentecostal membership is thus rather transient. The male is more restless and fickle than the female. He will join a church, feel some emotional excitement or release, then move on to the next storefront to satisfy his needs, perhaps with the jaded conviction that religion can do nothing for him. He searches for religious satisfaction much as he does for sexual satisfaction. Women are more faithful, stable, and monogamous —in religion as in sex. It is for this reason and others (including the mysterious complexities of theology) that churches appealing to women usually have greater staying power. A contrast is

Judaism, a religion of notable longevity, which is even more male-centered than the Christian.

Conversions to evangelical Protestantism among Puerto Ricans often begins on the Island, among the impoverished rural *campesinos* whom Catholicism seldom reaches. In one Puerto Rican village, I saw two Pentecostal churches within a half mile of each other, serving not more than two hundred families. The Pentecostal does for the Puerto Rican some of the things the Black Muslims do for Negroes. It emphasizes the virtues of self-help, thrift, industry, self-control—virtues that may lead to upward mobility. Unlike the Muslims, it does not use protest or race conflict as organizing devices.

About this time each year a report is given to parishioners on the Spiritual and Financial condition of the Parish.

Spiritually, St. _____ is improving steadily. The Legion of Mary has done good work. The number of Communions, the attendance at week-day Masses and at the Spanish Novena to Our Lady of Perpetual Help, are consoling. Of course, Mass attendance on Sundays and Holydays can still be improved, and there are still many marriages that could be rectified.

Financially, St. _____ is a headache. While our parishioners are not well-to-do, still the average weekly contribution to the Church, with a little planning and thought, could be much improved, at least to the cost of a ticket to the movies. Many of our parishioners could and should give one dollar in the Sunday offering. . . . This is doubly true of the parents of our school children, who receive more than they give. The major portion of our expenses are school expenses, and even if tuition is paid, the cost of schooling for a child is much greater—more than double. . . . With the opening of new projects within the confines of the parish, we may be forced to limit entrance of children to our schools to those living within the limits of the parish, and since even these can not all be

*accommodated, to those who are good parishioners and fulfill
their religious obligations of Mass on Sunday, . . .*
—BULLETIN OF AN EAST HARLEM ROMAN CATHOLIC CHURCH

There are more churches in East Harlem than all other public
and private institutions combined, except business—135 in all.
More adults engage in church affairs than in any other organized
activity.

Despite their numbers and potential influence, most churches
stand outside the social action scene. Religion's domain in East
Harlem is still more spiritual than social. Only the new middle
class white Protestant churches are deeply committed to community action. All churches, it is agreed, have to run to stay
even, and many people remain "unchurched."

The majority religion in East Harlem is Roman Catholicism.
In the area roughly from 98 to 135 Streets, 57 per cent are
Catholic; about 35 per cent, Protestant; 7 per cent, Jewish; and
the rest, "other."* Most people seem to be nominal church
members.

The Catholic church "stays to itself" and doesn't "do much
in the community," the non-Catholics in East Harlem said. Some
even claimed the church was too accepting of the underworld
"Cosa Nostra" groups that blossomed in the Italian days. A gulf
of unfamiliarity, some rivalry and suspicion, and the ethnic split
between Italians and Negroes separate the two halves of
Christianity in the area. One Italian leader, who has spent most
of his life in East Harlem, had never heard of a major Catholic
church—the only Spanish Catholic church in the area.

Catholicism is still based in the Italian community, though
most parishes are now mixed Italian and Puerto Rican. Virtually
every Italian child is enrolled in parochial school. Negroes are
going to the Catholic schools in noticeable numbers for the same
reason—to escape the racially segregated public schools. Puerto
Ricans tend to go to public rather than parochial schools.

* Central Harlem (almost all Negro) is by contrast 19 per cent Roman
Catholic, 76 per cent Protestant, 3 per cent Jewish, and the rest "other."

In both race and religion, Puerto Ricans are a swing group, part Negro and part white, part Catholic and part Protestant. While East Harlem's Protestant churches are intent on making Puerto Rican converts, they long ago gave up on proseletizing among Italians. The Italian heresy has tended to be more "radical" and political than Protestant, though La Guardia was a Protestant. Puerto Ricans, being less firmly tied to Catholicism than previous migrants, are more open to conversion.

Half the Italians are only nominal Catholics, it is said, and the Puerto Ricans are even more detached. A gentle people, slow to protest, Puerto Ricans often complain about Catholicism on the Island. They say the church is "all take and no give"; that it does not "do things for people" or "help people in time of need"; that there aren't enough priests; and that the priests come from Spain and do not understand the people. The church's absence from the rural village and the fact that most East Harlem Puerto Ricans come from such villages perhaps explain as well as anything their estrangement from Catholicism.

They also complain about the church's involvement in Island politics and its unsuccessful skirmishes with Governor Muñoz over the popular issues of birth control and separation of church and state. At the same time many are convinced that Catholicism had made their culture a gentle and compassionate one, and the people serene and unobsessed by material pursuits.

Catholic priests in East Harlem are almost exclusively Italian, with some Irish. The ecumenical movement in the church and the new militancy found in other urban places have not yet reached East Harlem. Some say the priests do not take part because they do not want to risk public competition with others. The church remains aloof from the larger community. And the community returns the favor. The church and the Italians are usually thought of as "them" by the white Protestants. Though the White Protestants are eager to integrate the community racially, they seem more happy than displeased that the Italians (and their church) are leaving, even though the Italians are the only major white group remaining.

In East Harlem the Protestant churches gained members as Italians moved out and Negroes moved in.* Most Protestant evangelical churches meet in storefronts and are nearly as transient as their congregations. At last count, there were 9 Roman Catholic and 121 Protestant churches. In addition there were two Orthodox churches and three Jewish synagogues. In 1959–1960 there were 54 Protestant churches in East Harlem with Puerto Rican congregations; in 50 of them Spanish was the primary language of the church.

While more than one-third of the churches in Central Harlem are Baptist, the largest group in East Harlem, Baptists, run neck and neck with the Pentecostals. Each has 21 churchs. In addition there are 6 Churches of God, 5 Apostolic, 4 Methodist, 4 Assemblies of Christian Churches, and 35 unclassified.

In Manhattan, and elsewhere in the city, Protestants are clustered at opposite ends of the status totem pole—the Park Avenue Whites and Central Harlem Negroes, the highest and the lowest incomes. Of the 726 Protestant churches in Manhattan, half are in Harlem and East Harlem.† Almost two out of every three

---

* Nationally they have not done well recently. In 1962 Protestant membership gain (0.77 per cent) did not keep up with the population gain (1.6 per cent). In 1950, Protestants were 38.8 per cent of the population; in 1962 they were only 34.9 per cent. At the same time the Roman Catholic membership gain was 2.3 per cent, and the Catholic proportion of the population has increased from 16 per cent in 1926 to 18.9 per cent in 1950 and 23.6 per cent in 1962.

† Only 53 of the 726 Protestant churches in Manhattan have membership of more than 1,000, and these account for 50 per cent of affiliated Protestants. Median membership of Protestant churches in East Harlem is 100 to 150. Total membership is estimated at 25,000. Active church membership in almost all denominations seems overwhelmingly female, largely middle-aged and over. No records are kept, however, of vital statistics on sex, race, or age.

Protestant affiliation in East Harlem shot up in 1950 (an increase of 46 per cent over 1945), declined slightly by 1955 (a loss of 0.6 per cent), and grew again in 1960 (a 13 per cent gain). Most of the gain derives from the influx of Negroes. In *Central* Harlem affiliation declined considerably by 1960, as against the 1945 figure. During that period Central Harlem experienced a parallel loss of population as Negroes moved out of this area. Protestant membership grew more in East Harlem between 1945 and 1960 than in any neighboring Manhattan community.

Protestants were almost half of New York's population in 1900. By 1957 they had declined to 23 per cent. At the same time the Catholic population

Manhattan Protestants are Negroes (63 per cent). Only 6.2 per cent are Puerto Ricans.

The Catholic population of East Harlem is about the same proportion as the city's—about half the total. Protestants are 35 per cent, compared with 23 per cent in the city. Except for its small Jewish population (which in the city is one-third the total), the area more nearly resembles the whole city than do most of New York's slums.

The scarcity of Jewish residents deprives East Harlem of much active, experienced, and progressive leadership. Some of the deficit is made up by the participation of a few Jewish outsiders in East Harlem organizations. Increasingly, as Jewish leaders replace old-guard white Protestants, New York's neighborhood houses are moving into vigorous social and political action. Middle class Jewish participation in Reform Democratic party politics (in this case replacing the old-line Tammany Irish and Italian Catholic groups) may also inject new vitality into the Democratic party and New York politics.

Individuals from the Jewish community have made remarkable contributions—mainly through forceful social action—in uplifting and organizing East Harlem. Ethnic style is sometimes an obstacle. Some say that because the Jewish style is "different" (vigorous and more outspoken) acceptance on both sides is seldom total. Some Jewish activists claim they do not feel at home in East Harlem. They get impatient with people who will not speak up for themselves, voice their grievances, or protest against injustice. Some say they continually confront—not anti-Semitism—but a drowsy acceptance of old clichés. Negroes, becoming real "protestant" and upwardly mobile, are perhaps moving closer to the Jewish style than the unusually amiable and accepting Puerto Ricans.

The biggest social action news in East Harlem in recent years has been made by the affluent white Protestant. The

increased from 35 per cent in 1900 to 49 per cent—or almost half the population in 1957. The Jewish population of the city declined from a high of 31 per cent in 1910 to 27 per cent in 1957.

Protestant "missions"—particularly the Friends and the East Harlem Protestant Parish—have rivaled crime as a subject of press discussion. The profuse journalistic attention to East Harlem has settled on delinquency, dope, and white Protestantism.

A white Protestant clergy in slum areas is indeed newsworthy. Though Negroes, the most depressed group in the nation, are Protestants, the white Protestant churches have been notoriously indifferent to the spiritual and social welfare of their black brethren. Perhaps no greater gulf stretches between people of the same religion as between white and Negro Protestants. The two have often been at opposite poles—financially, culturally, politically.

The limited Protestant offering to Negroes has usually been charity in one or another form, plus some lectures on hard work and self-help. Social action, politics, organization of the poor have often been regarded as ill-mannered, divisive, and threatening.

White Protestants suburbanized faster than other groups, moving far away from the Negro and white poor who crowded the central city. They have, thus, been quite out of touch, geographically and culturally, with the Negroes who share their faith. In contrast the Catholic immigrants moved in next door to other Catholic groups (as the Puerto Ricans moved into East Harlem's Italian blocks). They shared the same physical and spiritual facilities, despite the running disputes over who was to get what.

Against this background the spectacle of Protestant action in East Harlem is seen. A significant phase of the Negro protest movement has been the visible emergence of "respectable" white Protestantism on the side of Negro social action. It has favored restraint, but it has also favored action. Jewish and many Catholic groups long ago gave support to the protests of the impoverished; but white Protestantism—except at the National Council of Churches' top level—has stayed pretty much on the other side of the fence, guarding its property. Catholics, Negroes, and Jews have generally voted together and moved together, sharing a common have-not ideology, if not status. In recent years the centralized authority of the Catholic Church came down heavily on the side of civil rights. Yet Protestants—particularly the "democratic" sects—often remained conservative and aloof. After Birmingham, Protestant churches entered the civil rights arena in earnest and en masse.

Church social action in East Harlem springs out of a subcurrent of liberal and democratic-socialist sentiment in the white Protestant clergy, a current that produced Norman Thomas and Reinhold Niebuhr. Thus, the ministers offer a triple surprise: their fair-haired aspect, their importance in this dark-skinned Catholic community, and their political deviation from the conservative norms of "respectable" Protestantism. The East Harlem Protestant Parish, seat of white Protestantism in the area, is not simply middle class, as are most of the "agency" people and other whites. In life style it is more nearly upper class. It combines two contrasting qualities: status and "militancy." Many of the Parish ministers and those at its periphery are from the upper reaches of cultivated America. Some come from families of wealth and social status. Many have been educated at "quality" schools and have a mark of cultured distinction about them, mixed with a contrasting zeal for social and political action. Some did field work in East Harlem while attending Union Theological Seminary.

That the Parish is more upper than middle class is not unexpected. *Noblesse oblige* takes firmer root in the secure upper class. The traditional Tory often empathizes with the poor more than does the "classical" middle class liberal. He can afford to be more accepting. Besides, his speech, life style, and moral code are usually more natural, less puritanical, and therefore closer to the ways of the poor. He can afford to wear a shiny suit, frayed shirt, and worn shoes; he has no need to demonstrate his superiority. The Tory is often as much drawn to the poor as he is repelled by the established middle class merchant and fearful of the rising middle class. Not surprisingly, in politics many "aristocrats" have chosen to enter the Democratic party rather than the Republican. The ministers in East Harlem are far from being Tories, but some are of this social class.

Parish ministers do not want to be written about. Writers, they say, have hurt both the Parish and the community. The complaint is that the sensational is overplayed—murder, rape, addiction, prostitution—giving the area an undeserved bad name.

Some people in East Harlem are sensitive about their own and the community's public image. They do not want the community regarded as a zoo, a menagerie, or a jungle. Merchants and landlords are, as always, more concerned than others about the public face of East Harlem. A poor image is bad for business. It is also bad for Protestantism, it would seem.

Some reporters have portrayed parish ministers as martyred missionaries living amidst squalor and giving their life to the conversion of "the heathen." The image is neither accurate nor helpful. The Parish's desire to be left alone must be respected, but not its rejection of the *positive* attention from outsiders that East Harlem so desperately needs. A central strategy of white middle class leadership is to attract more of their own kind to the community, to give it some ethnic and economic balance. Outsiders should, then, be encouraged to participate in the community and learn about it.

Two of the most important features of Parish operations are the emphasis on social and political action rather than religious revivalism, and the requirement that all ministers live in the area.

The poor seem to need devils, someone to blame. A favorite devil is the outsider, the absentee overlord, the one who is not really "one of us." Though suspicion of nonresidents in East Harlem has become exaggerated and pervasive, it is rooted in a history of abuse and neglect.

Residence in the community means that the ministers are

full-time citizens, intimate with the area's people and problems and involved in their common fate. Residence distinguishes the ministers from social workers in East Harlem, most of whom are nonresidents and have no personal stake in the community.

The original formulation of the Parish's political philosophy was:

—Neutrality in politics is a myth.
—God is not only concerned with the soul of man but with the whole of man. He wills a just social order. His followers are there-fore obligated to participate actively in seeking social justice.
—Political institutions are sinful, but so are all human institutions.
—We are confident only that it is God's will that we should work through all means possible, including political parties . . . to cast off oppression and to seek justice for all.

Politics is a dirty game, they said: We must get in and help clean up the dirt. The Reform Democratic movement ran candidates for office and opposed "old-line" Italian (Catholic) clubs. With Parish and other support, the Reform movement swept East Harlem, and Puerto Ricans, Negroes, and white Protestants took power from the vanishing Italian minority. Don Benedict, a founder of the Parish, unsuccessfully ran for the city council in 1953. Now the assemblyman (state repre-sentative) in East Harlem is a Puerto Rican, Carlos Rios, who was formerly a Parish lay minister. The Parish has changed its political tack. It is no longer officially partisan, though it still stresses political action, and individual ministers are deeply involved in Reform politics.

"Opposition to the inactive Donovan [congressman] and support for the liberal Democrat Casper Citron," Bruce Kenrick wrote, "meant a fight against some of the most firmly en-trenched Tammany clubs in the city; for example, it was re-ported that in the club nearest the Parish office, over three hundred persons were beholden to it for their jobs; and such a number, with their friends and relatives, represented a powerful political machine on election day." Election districts in the Parish were organized under a captain and the vote turned out. Now one Parish minister is responsible for following all legislation affecting East Harlem.

A group ministry was set up. Instead of operating as independent agents, as relatively freewheeling Protestant individualists and entrepreneurs, the ministers in the group shared the same rules, work, and style of life. The group set disciplines for itself: Devotional—time each day for prayer, readings, etc.; economic—pay to ministers according to need, not qualifications; vocational—submission of work for criticism by the group; political—hammer out political and legislative positions, then work for those positions. They were together, as they hoped the community one day would be.

"The working out of the disciplines," Kenrick said, ". . . slowly overcame the suspicions of their neighbors that the three founding ministers were engaged on a project to study the people of the slums, or else were a part of a Communist racket to get control of the area (why else should college graduates come and live in a place like East Harlem?)"

The group grew from three to eighteen members in six years, and was said to have a surplus of first-class applicants. Some have felt in recent years that the group is too large, too established, and too top-heavy with administration. As the group grew into a sizable and compatible community, it tended to seal itself off from the outside, some said. ". . . Coffee drinking was now done more with like-minded Group members than with the laity. The Group had tended to become the focus of our social life," Kenrick writes. ". . . Not only did the Group tend to become a psychological barrier between its members and the laity; it often formed a frustrating physical barrier, which imprisoned them in a multitude of staff meetings when they might have been out on the streets or in the homes, helping meet their parishioners' needs." One minister resigned: "The Group convenes itself an improvident number of times in the course of even a week."

Some who are close to the Parish say it is much less daring and militant than it once was, and rather more involved in social work than in social action. The Parish now has an administrator, and office building, and much paper work. Some feel it is too "institutionalized" and that the ministers should spend more time with the people, in the streets and in the storefronts, and less time at their desks. The militants feel it should "mobilize" rather than "minister" to people, as it once set out to do.

Parish ministers are seen at most community meetings. They are active in school affairs. They operate a center for work with drug addicts, a study club, and various youth programs. The Parish has stimulated interest in voter registration and political action and tried to upgrade, through citizen action, the quality of public school education. It has devoted itself in an unassuming but vital way to real problems in the real world.

"And yet, the God of the churches which East Harlem knows," said a former Parish minister, "stays in celestial splendor far above this earth, but the God of this life is Vito Marcantonio and his Kingdom is the American Labor Party. Obviously the God who can get the plumbing fixed becomes the center of faith for the great majority."

The Parish has good plumbing. By its very presence it has helped create a more socially mixed community.

THE CHURCH MILITANT

One of East Harlem's most eloquent and earnest churchmen is Rev. Melvin Schoonover, pastor of the Chambers Memorial Baptist Church in East Harlem. Schoonover, once a minister of the East Harlem Parish, quit the Parish because he was assigned too much paper work. He wanted action. Though he cannot walk and moves about in a wheel chair, he went looking for tough work and found it—in a top corner of East Harlem, the Triangle, an area so filled with troubles and hard-to-move tenants that major urban renewal may be impossible there.

The Triangle has no public housing and little of anything but trouble. As Schoonover said, it is as though the social services that flood some areas of East Harlem ended at East 125 Street, at the door of the Triangle. Its population, mainly Negro and desperately poor, gets less attention from social workers than less needy places in the area.

Some sparks shot out of the Triangle when the City Planning Commission announced that it would hold public hearings on eighteen areas in the city considered suitable for urban renewal. The Triangle was one. The announcement sounded an alert. Demolition of Triangle housing and relocation of residents were threatened. Melvin Schoonover went to the mimeograph machine. Some three thousand copies of a leaflet were passed out in the neighborhood, along with a map of the housing doomed to demolition and a call to a meeting.

People came, about one hundred of them, a sensational turnout for the Triangle. Bad as it is, the Triangle is home to many people, and they do not want to be dispossessed.

At the meeting, "City Hall" was denounced, but some of the older church fathers assured people they need not worry: "We'll take care of everything." Comforted, the meeting broke. Half the audience had left before Rev. Schoonover was able to call them back to order. Business was not finished. Everything was not "taken care of."

"We've said the city is a dirty dog, but can't we *do* something?" he asked. An *ad hoc* committee was set up. Someone said, "The city will clobber us with figures, so we should have our own." The result of all this was a comprehensive neighborhood study. Neighbors did the first interviews themselves; then college students came in and interviewed some five hundred people. "From the beginning," the minister said, "because we didn't know any better, we decided we had to do it ourselves."

About 24 per cent of the families said they wanted to move; 76 per cent said they wanted to stay. Nearly everyone wanted better housing, most didn't know where they would move if they had to leave.

Rents were remarkably low. Of 160 responses, 61 per cent

said they paid less than $40 per month rent; 35 per cent paid less than $30. Only 10 per cent paid more than $80. One person owned his own home. Almost everyone said they would pay more rent to get better housing, and nearly a quarter said they would be interested in cooperative housing.

At the same time, known cases of overcrowded housing amounted to 75 per cent of the total. Tearing down the Triangle, it was concluded, would only cause further shortage and more crowding in the city. Many of the residents had already been moved one or more times from renewal sites. Living in the area also were a substantial number of single or elderly people who would have special trouble finding housing. Like most slums, the Triangle contained an excess of people at both age extremes—the very young and the very old—those in the middle range having escaped.

Incidental to its purpose the study also showed that federal census figures greatly underestimated the population in this and perhaps other crowded slums. The 1960 census reported 6,100 people in the Triangle. In the self-study in 1961—which involved a house-to-house canvass by trusted neighbors, not a sampling by suspect strangers—the total came to 10,000.

An excess of "problem families" seemed to make relocation impossible. Besides, the citizen report said: "Even if the city could guarantee 'decent, safe, and sanitary' housing to everyone displaced by urban renewal, the city's policy is unsatisfactory because it does not include any element of choice for the persons affected."

When the renewal board looked at the figures the community had put together and saw the citizen reaction, it decided to table for the time its proposal to raze the housing in the area and put in industry.

The threat from "City Hall" was the fuse Melvin Schoonover used to ignite the Triangle to new activity and unity. People came to meetings, protested, spoke to their neighbors, joined in the common task of rebuffing the invaders. A respected citizens group, the Triangle Community Association, was formed.

"The Association," the report said, "is making concerted attempts to upgrade its neighborhood, in spite of massive resistance on the part of the owners of dwellings concerned, indifference and fear on the part of some of the families residing in the area, and indifference and outright hostility to their efforts on the part of various city agencies. In addition, there is a long record of indifference on the part of political organizations, who are often willing to take the credit for improvements made but rarely willing to lift a finger prior to accomplishment of the task.

"The citizens of the community are rapidly learning that apparently the only way to obtain action and protection is to band together and exert political pressure. The callous way in which citizens are treated by the city in its administrative, legislative, and judicial capacities and the extent to which they are victimized by landlords and political groups furnish ample evidence to support this position."

The final document presented to the Board of Estimate was criticized as being too hostile. "You should have seen the original," Schoonover said, "I toned it down a lot." The document was a creation of Triangle citizens, and was given only mechanical assistance by the experts. "We are not stupid," said Schoonover.

A white man in a wheel chair, Melvin Schoonover somehow blended into the Negro and Puerto Rican landscape of the Triangle. He talks straight, to the point, speaks of action and self-help, and does not cloud the listener with metaphysics. The facts of life in the Triangle are stark. He does not cover them over. Some call him an angry man, angry about the abuse and neglect of the poor. His anger is not bitter or hostile. Let the "leadership" stand back for a change, he says, and let the community come through. "Stop putting out grass fires. Help light them."

"We shouldn't convince them they should be like us. Let them decide what *they* want to do."

Much is expected of the churches. They are the only formal organizations in which many of East Harlem's poor participate. How much have they helped? All have given comfort (however temporary), a meeting place, some social service; and a few have sunk their teeth into social issues.

The Catholic church in East Harlem has lived beside abject poverty and need for many years. Some of the churches, striking in their beauty and rich ornamentation, are the only jewels in East Harlem, but they seem to shine little light on the poor. In other slum communities priests and church have taken strong leads in social reform; not so in East Harlem.

But at least the Catholic church has been there. Before Don Benedict came with the Parish, only one Protestant church served 40,000 people in East Harlem, and that was closed except for five hours a week. Even among the more enlightened Protestant groups, social work and efforts to prop up individuals one by one has often been a genteel substitute for social action. Churches seldom make revolutions. Mainly they offer peace to the oppressed. The Marxian assertion that religion is the opiate of the poor is far from much of the reality of East Harlem. Still, much religious effort goes into quieting unrest and tranquilizing the searching spirit rather than giving it new direction.

There is not a single Negro church in East Harlem. These might have helped stimulated self-help and protest as they have other places. Most Negroes in the area go to church in Central Harlem. Even there the Negro church is divided and troubled. "Often we do not accomplish our objectives because of division," said one Central Harlem minister. "There is no longer a united voice. Labor leads for labor; the political powers have divided themselves. There is no one entity. This is Harlem's weakness. There is no group that I can think of that exercises an adequate amount of power. Our community is so complex and our problems are so tremendous that the groups feel inadequate, and as a result do nothing. This accounts for our inertia. There is no willingness to pool resources. There is no single group that can speak for Harlem."

Much the same could be said for East Harlem. It is split into three ethnic sections, themselves splintered, and with only loose lines of communication between them.

Such as it is, much of the "capital" of the poor is invested in the church. The total value of Protestant church land and property in Upper Manhattan (mainly Central and East Harlem) was estimated at $65 to $70 million. Expenditures in one recent year were $3.5 to $4 million for current expenses and between $500,000 and $600,000 for benevolent programs. Of course, much outside church money is also invested in the slum. At least one of the Catholic churches in East Harlem was reported by a knowledgeable source to have had a recent annual budget of $300,000.

It is interesting to speculate what profits might be, in worldly goods, if this "capital" had been invested in business and job-producing efforts—or in social rather than spiritual revival. "The Irish of New York and elsewhere," writes Daniel P. Moynihan, "have made a tremendous sacrifice for their church. They have built it from a despised and proscripted sect of the eighteenth century to the largest religious organization of the nation, numbering some 43,851,000 members in 1963. This is incomparably the most important thing they have done in America. But they have done it at a price. In secular terms, it has cost them dearly in men and money. A good part of the surplus that might have gone into family property has gone to building the church. This has almost certainly inhibited the development of the solid middle-class dynasties that produce so many of the important people in America."*

* Nathan Glazer and Daniel Patrick Moynihan, *Beyond the Melting Pot,* Cambridge, Mass.: M.I.T. Press and Harvard University Press, 1963.

Whatever religion's shortcomings, no viable alternative ideology is offered people of East Harlem. Churches cannot be criticized too harshly for doing inadequately what others are not doing at all. What might have helped East Harlem most is the evocation of an angry Jehovah and his prophets. What it got was mostly talk of the gentle Jesus. Each has a place and a time; both are needed in the slum.

7

I know of no safe depository of the ultimate powers of the society but the people themselves; and if we think them not enlightened enough to exercise their control with a wholesome discretion, the remedy is not to take it from them, but to inform their discretion.
—JEFFERSON

Power Structures and Vacuums

There are two icebergs in East Harlem: The "overworld" (landlords, business, finance) and the "underworld." No one knows much about either. Many suspect that both wield great hidden power.

Private landlords own most of the land and property in East Harlem, including two out of three housing units. They own all the slums. The public housing is all at least "decent," however stark. The private owners appear to be mainly speculators and big financial institutions—the mortgage holders and those whose business is real estate. Relatively few slum buildings are held by "little guys." Two individuals are said to have rather extensive holdings in East Harlem. One runs a business there and lives elsewhere. Another lives in an elegant house in the area.

It is not known how much big business and finance affect major decisions about East Harlem. It *is* known that these "owners" greatly influence government and public decisions, that they generally oppose public spending and policies favoring the poor and support policies favoring landlord, employer, merchant, or money lender.

The second iceberg, the underworld, is even less visible. None of the social agency people seem to know much about it, even though Cosa Nostra is a local East Harlem product. It is widely believed that the peddlers of numbers, drugs, and other addictive forms of escape have much payoff influence with other powers and that the over- and underworlds have much in common. Suspicions rather than proof are usually offered, but it is in the nature of such power that it is hidden and that it defies detection and evidence.

The "pushers" and peddlers are said to be everywhere. Recreation leaders almost had to close down at least one summer play street because the peddlers, according to an East Harlem detective, did not want to be watched by a street full of kids and do-gooders. CORE block organizers say the first thing they must do is identify and step around the underworld characters. These peddlers, it is claimed, do not want the community organized, at least not by anyone but themselves.

Power makes the community's wheels spin, skid, or stop. It is for this reason that solutions for the poor lie in their uncovering the secrets of power: What it is, how it operates, who has it, how to get it. The secrets are very well hidden; in fact, few things are further out of reach of the social scientist's research tools.

In recent years it has become fashionable with some people to dismiss as a rather paranoid delusion the poor man's search for the "power structure." "Everyone has power," they contend. It is clear, nonetheless, that in the community, as in a business or any organization, some people have much more "say" than others. In the community (the social organization) these lines of power and status are simply more twisted and concealed than in the business organization.

In a sense, community power is rather like a submarine. Its survival and strength depend on its secrecy. When it is spotted, depth charges may sink it.

As for popular and positive power that might help melt the two hidden icebergs or sink the subs, very little of it can be found in East Harlem. The power of the people is not developed. That's why East Harlem is a slum. The main source of outside power to which the slum can appeal for aid is government. Usually the appeal is to city government because it is closer and more responsive than state government. It is for this reason that politics and the vote are so essential in the slum.

Like almost all slums, East Harlem votes heavily Democratic. Until the reform movement took over the Democratic party in East Harlem, it had been led by the "old line," which was based on a vanishing and weak Italian vote.

Social workers were content, as usual, to work with the powers that be and build on their strengths. When the reformers came in, the Italians gave ground to the Puerto Ricans, Negroes, and white Protestants. The social workers were caught in the middle of this power transition. The Italian leaders felt that the social workers did not give them enough support, but many reformers felt that influential social workers were too close to the old "machine."

What there is of a visible power structure in East Harlem is a strange one. I certainly did not expect to find among so many impoverished migrants that middle class white Protestants would have so much influence. It should not be a surprise. The dominance of white Anglo-Saxon Protestants has been a pervasive reality in American life, uncovered in repeated studies of small towns, the metropolis, and national power structures. So it is in Spanish Harlem.

Perhaps the most influential community leaders are social workers—one in particular, a white Protestant. Another top stratum of influentials is the white Protestant clergy. One of the most active (and some say the most effective) political leader is a white Protestant. And some of East Harlem's top non Anglo-Saxon leaders have also been Protestant: Fiorello La Guardia (an Italian Protestant) and Carlos Rios (leading Puerto Rican assemblyman and a Protestant).

Most of the white Protestants in East Harlem are strongly identified with the reform group in the Democratic party. In New York City the reformers are essentially a coalition of middle class Protestants and Jews, joined against the "old-line" Italian and Irish Catholic working class. In Manhattan, the reformers have gained so much ground that even Catholic Mayor Robert Wagner has given them some nods. In East Harlem the reform group was built mainly by a Jewish leader (Mark Lane) and the Protestant clergy.

White Protestant leadership in East Harlem comes by default. As much as anything it is a product of the clannishness of Italian leaders and (except for Vito Marcantonio and a few others) a consequence of their failure to reach out a fraternal arm to the new residents, the Puerto Ricans and Negroes. It also comes out of a white Protestant heritage of accepted status and leadership. It is a leadership given them by their seniority in the New World and their influence on American life and culture. Even before the reformers came to East Harlem (in the post-Marcantonio days) Italian political leaders were often content to turn over decisions to the white Protestant social workers. They were considered suitable mediators between the immigrant community and the outside establishment.

Now Puerto Ricans also defer to the white Protestants. The Puerto Rican migrant, says Padilla, tends to venerate the white Protestant "American," preferring him to the Italian and Jewish immigrants who have been their neighbors.

The white Anglo-Saxon hegemony on the national scene is traditional and part of folk knowledge. It is not unexpected, then, to repeat the tradition of white Protestant Presidents and Vice Presidents, or to find a white Protestant governor (Nelson

Rockefeller) in New York State. It is less expected to find this hegemony in the city, among migrant Catholic, Jewish and dark Protestant minorities.

In New York City, where white Protestants are a rapidly vanishing breed, and are far out-numbered by the "immigrants," the mayor of the city is, ironically, an Anglo-Saxon (working class German—both the Angles and Saxons were German tribes) and a Catholic whose father converted from Protestantism. Another irony is that the first Jewish superintendent of schools in the city is, in church affiliation, a Protestant.

New York's Irish have had more political power than other immigrants. Though most Irish are Catholics, they are Celtic first cousins of the Anglo-Saxons and are English speaking. Irish political power held in East Harlem after the Irish vote was gone, mainly for that reason. The Irish looked like Anglo-Saxons and talked like them.

While Anglo-Protestant power has been traditionally conservative, in East Harlem it is generally liberal and militant. Their Protestant brethren among the Italian political leaders of prewar days were also liberal to radical.

The white Protestant hegemony has added, among other things, a certain sanitariness to the political and social life of East Harlem. Among their other virtues, the Protestants are very clean. Their presence may help familiarize the poor with this essential middle class virtue, for the middle class is nothing if not clean and tidy.

Most people who go to meetings in East Harlem are middle class or professional. Virtually all of the top *official* leaders in East Harlem are white or very light skinned. The Council for Community Planning in East Harlem, said by a City Planning Commission survey to be the most influential group in the community, is composed almost exclusively of white male professionals, businessmen, churchmen, social workers, school principals, etc. It often meets during the day when the average citizen could not attend if he wanted to.

The most influential person in East Harlem is believed to be a settlement house worker—male and white Anglo-Protestant—a man who has risen to this position because of personal abilities, long experience in the community, and familiarity with powers outside the community. The ethnic split among Italians, Puerto Ricans, and Negroes gives the outsider, especially an Anglo-Protestant, the advantage of ethnic neutrality.

Another influential leader also has roots in a settlement house. He is Italian and has been a man of stature in public life and in the affairs of the neighborhood over many decades. A political leader, not a social worker, his role in the community is limited by the fact that the settlement house with which he is associated is an Italian oasis in a changing neighborhood.

Whites dominate most organizations. At meetings, for example, of the Mayor's Local Planning Board, a leading community group, whites preside, compose most of the audience, do most of the talking, make most of the decisions. Some whites are aware of this and consciously try to stand back and let others come through. One white parent leader has a system; she lets Negroes and Puerto Ricans talk first. After their discussion is exhausted, she lets the whites speak. Holding back is unnatural and rather difficult. Whites, many of whom are superbly educated and fluent, have to restrain themselves while others "make their own mistakes." In East Harlem whites often talk about this problem. They want others to speak up, come to meetings, take leadership, but they also, quite naturally, want to speak out themselves and influence policy.

> *We set out to destroy the old power structure* [*the Italian political "machine"*] *but we found there was a parallel power structure still standing—the social workers.*
>
> —A YOUNG MILITANT

The parallel power structure remains. It probably will weave in the wind, take new shapes, and stay upright.

The militant whites want fast action. They feel that social

workers move too slowly and are too high handed, that they sit on dissent and discourage mass participation. "They try to cast the community in their own image," one militant said. "They want things better, but they want to determine what is better— no trouble, smooth things over, keep the peace!" Another militant said, "All the helping agencies have been engaged in a conspiracy for some time to convince people that they are powerless. The church dispenses charity. It wants people to be subservient and grateful. The people have been persuaded they are powerless." One East Harlem minister insists that the people are well able to lead themselves: "The people are not nearly so irresponsible as we think they are—nor so apathetic. There *is* social organization. There *are* black leaders, though they may not be regarded as leaders by outsiders. They have a tremendous amount of strength. They help one another. The community is not devoid of leadership or responsibility."

The helping agencies, it is said, deal with problems that are often not the most pressing concerns. "If you have a corn growing on your toe and can't walk, you can't be concerned about a cancer growing in your intestines." The people are honest, as one militant said: "There is relatively little hypocrisy here; that's one nice thing about the area. Ask them, and they'll tell you straight what they want."

Ultimately, power has to be political; what is needed has to come through government. Some of the leading social workers, the militants claim, are horrified at overt political action. Their rules of "fair play" are conciliation and influence. They think of politics as "dirty" and contaminating. They think it is not genteel to use political pressure. "Gentility is a way of life with them."

Let the people take power, say the militants. Encourage grass fires. If a group has a grievance get them to do something about it—and set a few fires while you're at it.

The civil rights movement has made things easier, they feel. People have begun to feel their oats and question whether they need to be the way they are: "We'll make mistakes, and many of the things we'll do will not be very good at all. But the people are growing out of childhood and need to make their own mistakes. Help people to clarify what they think about issues. Help them express themselves and organize to achieve what they want. The people want to become a part of the American dream."

The new militants speak of the "social work cabal." They see it as a thrombosis that is stopping the circulation of blood in the community. Social workers are like others. All establishments, even one so benign as East Harlem's, try to hold onto their seats. Yet they usually spawn those who will unseat them. Social workers, if they are doing a good job, encourage community leaders who grow up and want to take over. In East Harlem, social workers and others created Franklin Plaza, the middle income home of many of the new militants. Now they have to step aside for a time and let the protest and social action come through. Some social workers resist it, some welcome it, most are outside or uncertain. A few think that the new agitation is a shooting star that will flash and be gone. They are probably right. Already protest, having won some major points, is turning to more advanced stages of community effort.

The social worker is an easy target, sometimes too easy. Like other "public servants" (the teacher, policeman, etc.), the social worker is an alien emissary of the middle class world, put into the slum to do good and keep order. Usually he is not doing much to correct poverty—nor to create it either. The social worker did not make the slum; still he is sometimes resented for his patronage and abused because he is close at hand.

On the other hand, social workers (in general) need to be goaded into action. They have stood on the sidelines when they should have been in the ring. As Dr. Kenneth Clark's Harlem project report said: "Most of the suggestions of agency personnel were geared to remediation, in the sense of treatment of individuals, rather than problem solving and social action. The

generally peripheral, if not trivial, perspective of Central
Harlem agencies appears to be pervasive in the social services
field."

Others have also aimed straight at the social workers' soft
spots:

The day after the bomb fell, the doctor was out binding up
radiation burns. The minister prayed and set up a soup kitchen
in the ruined chapel. The policeman herded stray children to the
rubble heap where the teacher had improvised a classroom. And
the social worker wrote a report; since two had survived, they held
a conference on Interpersonal Relationships in a Time of Intensified
Anxiety States.—MARION K. SANDERS in *Harper's Magazine*

Social agencies need helpless people in order to have people to
help. Added to that is the fact that even the most open-minded
people can't accept the poor even as potential equals. The result is
that some workers, quite unconsciously, see their jobs as a sedative
for social ills rather than a good hard push toward change.—From
a speech by PRESTON WILCOX

Some of my friends in East Harlem said: "What can you see
of East Harlem looking out the window of 250 East 105 Street
[Union Settlement]?" They were saying I had a prosettlement
bias, and though I don't believe that's true, I can't bring myself
to criticize settlement workers or, for that matter, anyone living
or working in East Harlem. Agency people have flaws, and
some have big ones, but most of those I met in East Harlem
deserve more praise and less blame than they get.

Union Settlement has contributed a great deal to East Harlem
since 1895, when it opened its doors. It has done many of the
usual things and done them well: community centers, recreation, day care for children of working mothers, music school,
credit union, summer festival, tutorials, etc. More recently it
has tried to move out into community organization. At the top
levels it has organized and worked through the East Harlem
Council for Community Planning and the Borough President's

Planning Board. At the grass roots, it has worked through the East Harlem Project, a joint creation of Union and Johnson settlement houses.

The East Harlem Council was organized after the First World War and is the oldest neighborhood council in New York. It is an "organization of organizations"—of professionals and "leaders."

"This organization [the council] represents by far the most powerful, influential, organized, sophisticated and articulate leadership group in the community," said a report of the City Planning Commission. "It is closely associated with and financially supported by Union Settlement, whose Headworker is not only the Chairman of the Council but a strong influence on the Council's philosophy and program. The two or three people who represent the dominant forces behind the Council have these characteristics in common: they reside in places other than East Harlem; they are professionals; they have a similar point of view. . . . They are determined to see the community's development follow the course they consider most appropriate and desirable." The council is a network that "relates to all of the leaders and organizations in East Harlem." However, said the report, "There appears to be a sizable communication gap between it and the majority of the grass roots community who have no contact at all with the Council." The council "thinks of itself as committed to citizen participation, not only in word but in deed. . . . It has an enormous enrollment of community leaders and has proven it can assemble this group and guide its decision-making in a crisis. . . . The best access to the East Harlem community at present is secured through the Council."

There have been only one or two Negroes and Puerto Ricans on its twenty-six-member board, and meetings of the council have had only a thin sprinkling of dark skins.

Another top "leadership" group is the East Harlem Civic Association (no women and very few Negroes and Puerto

Ricans). Though there seems to be no official link with the council, it is said that the council tries to involve Italian leaders of the Civic Association in the affairs of the community. The association is called the strongest voice of the Italian community. Critics charge that the council itself is too close to the Italians.

The Planning Board in East Harlem, the community's liaison with the city (led by Bill Kirk of Union Settlement) holds its meetings in the evening and attracts more indigenous people than the council.

Another effort which Union initiated jointly with the Johnson and Henry Street settlements is the consumer education program. The three settlements sponsored the research on which the book *The Poor Pay More*, by David Caplovitz, a study of consumer habits was based.* The study found the vast majority of East Harlem residents to be insolvent financially or on the verge of it. The East Harlem Project assigned a worker to educate consumers on credit buying, shopping, credit unions and to set up service centers, issue an exchange service bulletin and do comparative shopping.

Like many New York settlements, Union was touched with the glamour of its alumni, including such people as Burt Lancaster. La Guardia Neighborhood House, East Harlem's Italian settlement, has had more politicians than film stars in its past—Fiorello La Guardia and Vito Marcantonio among others. Though La Guardia House is in transition now, trying to hold together the remnants of the Italian community and occupy the many Italian "senior citizens" who remain, it has had a sensationally colorful past. Commissioner Corsi, its director, is still active and interested, searching for ways to improve relations among Italians and Puerto Ricans.

I lived at La Guardia House for several months and worked with a group of preteen girls—not too successfully. It seemed to me that these girls were virtually closed to communication

* New York, Free Press of Glencoe, 1963.

with the outside world—especially with adults and non-Italians —and while I found working with them (that is, watching them dance, sing, play Ping-Pong) interesting, I usually felt like a superfluous and suspect stranger. This is not to say that others, trained in group work or closer to them in life style, could not penetrate this barrier of suspicion. The tradition of La Guardia House is male, Italian, liberal, Republican, and Protestant; I was outside the tradition.

Other settlements, also of great influence, are James Weldon Johnson, The Friends, and Casita Maria.*

Social workers in *private* agencies, because they have been around longer, seem to have more influence in East Harlem than workers in *public* agencies, who are far more numerous.†

A rough count of who's-who among professionals and business people at the top level—as listed in the East Harlem Project's directory—added up to a total of 194, as shown in the table below. This is the white collar "power structure." If these middle class people have exercised unusual influence, it was because nobody else would or did. They filled a vacuum.

East Harlem may be called a welfare state. Or, more properly, a "very little welfare" state. It has been driven to welfare and poverty by forces of the market place. Private builders would not go near low income housing. Private landlords neglected

---

* Dan Wakefield's *Island in the City* (Boston: Houghton Mifflin, 1959) describes some of the work of the Friends—an agency which the clothes-conscious Italians describe as "beatnik." The Friends are perhaps closer to the poor than the other settlements.

† In East Harlem there were 10 recreation centers, 1 home, and 1 social security office for the aged. There were 8 credit unions, 15 day care centers, 9 remedial reading centers, 9 adult education programs, 14 centers for unmarried mothers, 2 Youth Boards, 1 family planning center, and a number of disconnected medical and mental health services.

Including summer programs, there were 33 Parks Department playground workers. There were 39 community and recreation centers. Sixteen were attached to public schools, and the others were private, mainly church sponsored.

As for civic associations (which, unlike the agencies, were not usually operated by professionals with outside funds), there were some 26 in East Harlem, including many Puerto Rican hometown groups, such as the Luqillo Social Club.

Public school principals and board members	43
Day care directors	13
Clergymen	26
Bank managers and presidents	6
Public housing management	13
Hospital and health center directors	11
Library and museum heads	5
Merchants Association members	10
Private agency leaders	22
Public agency leaders	5
Senior citizen club workers	6
Police and Youth Board chiefs	10
Conservation and Area Services directors	4
Site businessmen at East River	6
Franklin Plaza Planning Board	10
Community centers	4
	194

their buildings and kept them as profitable slums. Government did what it could; it ripped up the slums and rebuilt. And it started to put on patches when some people objected to demolition.

Private medical care, expensive as it is, seldom reaches the poor. Government has tried to give some substitute medical service. East Harlem's poor are still much more likely to be sick and unattended than their middle class counterparts. The poor are more likely to be emotionally disturbed; yet private psychiatric care is far out of reach. Again, government has made a few, a very few, stabs at treatment. Private agencies and religious groups usually clear out of areas when the poor come in.

Underlying the poverty of the slums and all its symptoms: The private business economy has not supplied enough jobs. Only now, as it did during the depression, is government beginning to talk about putting some of the youthful jobless to work through training and job corps programs.

Especially in the slum, government is a mediating power between the poor and the rich, the impotent and the powerful, the unemployed and the employer. It tries to put the two together.

Government is also a substitute power. When the private system fails or breaks down, government may come forward, like a cosigner on a check, to make substitute payments.

In the slum—by default of the private system—public agencies govern rents and housing codes, provide schools, parks, police protection, welfare and public assistance, sanitary services, and some health care. Government has the power of life and death over a neighborhood. It can, through renewal, wipe it out (or move it elsewhere), leave it as it is, or fix it up. It provides direct services to the poor in every area except the most basic and important—jobs.

East Harlem has not been organized to make proper use of public services or to shape the policies of public agencies.

POWER AT THE POLLS

Politics is the poor man's bank roll. What the poor lack in financial power they can make up in voting power, since they are numerically strong.

In New York the poor are relatively impotent because many do not vote. The biggest obstacle to voting is New York's voter literacy test, required by the state constitution. This test disqualifies, or scares off, about half of the otherwise eligible Puerto Rican voters and large numbers of southern Negroes with limited education. New York is the only state outside the South that requires a literacy test, a device used historically to disfranchise the poor. States such as Texas, Arizona, New Mexico, Nevada, and California have bilingual provisions in the voting laws. New York does not.

New York's voting laws also make registration quite temporary and relatively very difficult. Those who miss an election now and then (more often the poor) are taken from the voting rolls and have to start over again. Long lines are also thrown up as obstacles. I for one have had to wait in line for more than two hours simply to change my voting address in New York.

In Central Harlem 56.8 per cent of the voting age population did *not* vote in 1960. In the district covering East Harlem, 53.6 per cent did *not* vote. These were among the highest percentages of nonvoters to be found anywhere in northern cities. In the one Republican district in Manhattan (John Lindsay's), the percentage of nonvoters was 39.4 per cent, high for a middle class district but low compared with low income districts. In Puerto Rico only 20 per cent of those who are of voting age do not vote. In the following table, the figures are for the percentage of the total voting age population that did *not* vote in 1960. Except for Baltimore, a city below the Mason-Dixon line, New York has the highest per cent of nonvoters.*

Baltimore	42.2%
New York City	42.2%
Kansas City (Mo.)	40.1%
Cleveland	38.6%
Newark	38.3%
St. Louis	38.0%
Boston	36.6%
San Francisco	35.6%
Milwaukee	33.6%
Cincinnati	33.2%
Los Angeles	32.7%
Pittsburgh	31.7%
Philadelphia	30.2%
Detroit	30.0%
Chicago	24.2%

At the time of the 1960 presidential election Manhattan had five congressmen: A Negro (Adam Clayton Powell), a white Anglo-Saxon Protestant (John V. Lindsay, the lone Republican), an Irishman (William Fitts Ryan), a Jew (Leonard Farbstein), and an Italian (Alfred Santangelo). After the 1960 census Manhattan lost one congressional seat because of a drop in population, and Santangelo was squeezed out of Manhattan and East Harlem, leaving Powell to represent East as well as Central Harlem. Though Negroes and Puerto Ricans are almost half

* A breakdown of voters by congressional district is shown in Appendix 2.

the population of Manhattan, they hold one out of the four congressional seats.

Adam Clayton Powell is now East Harlem's congressman— absentee congressman, some say. Other political representatives are: State Senator Jerome Wilson; City Councilman Robert Low; State Assemblymen José Ramos-Lopez, Carlos Rios, Frank Rossetti. All are white or light skinned, except Rios, who has a brown coloring. Even Powell is Caucasian in appearance. Often at political gatherings in East Harlem, not a single dark-skinned speaker will appear.

John Merli's Miami Democratic Club, across the street from Union Settlement, was and is the bulwark of Italian politics in East Harlem. "The Irish had to go," Merli said, "and I gotta go out sometime. I know that . . . I didn't have to run for the Council again, but I don't want to be bulldozed. The Puerto Rican people are going to take over. But that man [Mark Lane] is making a jungle out of this neighborhood."

The two most famous political leaders in East Harlem's past have been Italians—La Guardia and Marcantonio. La Guardia is the community's brightest star. He launched his political career as a Republican in 1914. "My knowledge of Italian and Yiddish came in handy," he said. "I rang doorbells and talked to the im-migrant families. At outdoor meetings I would wait until the regular political rally had ended, pull up in my Ford, gather a crowd and do my talking."

Vito Marcantonio came along a little later. La Guardia first spotted him when Marcantonio led a successful tenant's strike at the age of twenty. In 1924, as a law student at New York University, Marcantonio managed La Guardia's successful cam-paign for Congress in East Harlem. Like La Guardia, he spoke Italian and Yiddish, but in addition Marcantonio spoke East Harlem's new language, Spanish, a talent that helped make him a favorite of Puerto Rican voters. In 1934, after La Guardia be-came mayor, Marcantonio was elected to Congress in East Harlem on the Republican–City Fusion ticket. He served six terms in Congress. His name came to be prominently associated with both the underworld and the Communist party.

Thomas Luchese, head of one of New York's Cosa Nostra families according to Mafia informant Joseph Valachi, was an "old friend from East Harlem of the late Rep. Vito Marcantonio." When Luchese's son, Robert, went to West Point, Marcantonio made the necessary arrangements.* Those who worked with him in East Harlem report that Marcantonio was a close associate of such underworld figures as Johnny Dio.

His alleged associations with the Communist party were more damaging; and the Republican, Democratic, and Liberal parties finally joined together to defeat him in 1950. In 1951, Marcantonio's protégé, Manuel Medina, running on the American Labor party ticket, almost beat out Democrat John Merli for the City Council, pulling out a large vote among Puerto Ricans.

Then came Mark Lane, Democratic state assemblyman, young, Jewish, "radical," who managed to pull out sizable non-Italian votes in East Harlem.

"I never saw Marcantonio in my life," Lane said. "There is an old story that I was his first campaign manager—I'd have been about six years old at the time. But I am from his old district, and I can tell you his work in that community is not forgotten. I disagree with his foreign policy, but I believe that what he did in the community was admirable."

Mark Lane left East Harlem to run, unsuccessfully, for Congress in Manhattan's West Side.

A POLITICAL POSTSCRIPT

Sam Hirsch, who helped me a lot in East Harlem, is a politician by avocation. I ran in to him at a school meeting and then saw him everywhere I went. He is a walking example of what can happen to people, individually, when they get "involved" in politics. He admits that he used to be very shy and never could get up courage to talk to people. At eighteen he somehow got

---

* "The Five Lords of the Underworld," *Post*, October 15, 1964, p. 27.

involved in a Marcantonio campaign and went knocking on doors in East Harlem. "I was so petrified with fear at the thought of talking to strangers that, when the first person opened the door, I choked and nothing came out. I couldn't speak." Now he talks quite a bit. There was a period when he "felt badly" and was upset. "I had to pull myself out of it," he said, and he did just that—he went out and organized; it was his therapy and hobby. This personal knowledge of suffering left behind sympathy for the plight of others rather than bitterness at his own.

His support of reformers in East Harlem has been very effective—though his choice of some candidates would not have been my own. Employed at a desk job by the Chefs and Cooks Union, AFL–CIO, he spends almost every spare moment in politics. He laughs a lot (often at himself), telephones people, maintains an amazing network of contacts, and keeps many people in East Harlem informed and in touch with each other. It was my pleasure to spend a good deal of time with him in East Harlem.

BRUTALITY, COPS, CRIME

The slum's war with the world is waged against its available agents—social workers, schools, City Hall, slumlords—but above all against police.

When the Central Harlem "police brutality" riots of 1964 erupted, East Harlem only a few blocks away was quiet. Puerto Ricans, Negroes, Italians—eating *zoppolis* and riding ferris wheels at the street fair of Our Lady of Mount Carmel Church, had other things to do. East Harlem is poorer than Central Harlem, but it is, except for areas like the Triangle, an economic, not a racial, ghetto. This can make a critical difference. The light- and dark-skinned live there, and many freely mix. Unlike Central Harlem, much of it is in skin color, a mixed community, and racial tension is minimal. There is also less general hostility, since Puerto Ricans have it somewhat easier than Negroes, and more apathy and less organization among its stricken poor. These and other factors, minimize riotous violence.

Even in East Harlem the complaints about crime run a full range. It is said that there aren't enough police or enough protection, that the police are corrupt and as bad as the criminals— and that they are brutal, that they abuse the innocent along with the guilty and pick on minority groups. The police also have many defenders, and most people either don't have any experience with police or think that there are "good ones and bad ones."

Citizen comments, tape recorded on the streets of East Harlem after the 1964 summer riots (precipitated by the fatal police shooting of a fifteen-year-old Negro youth in mid-Manhattan) showed that, even in the relative safety of East Harlem's streets, feelings about the police run strong. One middle-aged Negro man said:

The police they really is too brutal—with the kids, or even with the colored people. I keep quiet, I got a family to support, so I got out of it. The killing of this kid, it stirred up a lot of people: It stirred up *me*, it stirred up our leaders, it stirred up all Negroes. Do you know what I mean?
I think that New York City should have a talk with the police commissioner and ask him to don't use too much brutality with the people. Use it if you have to use it. But as long as a man or a kid is willing to be under arrest, handle him with care. Don't shove him. Something should be did about it.
It's not safe in Harlem now. You don't know what the Police Department is going to do. They might shoot *anyone*. They're afraid. Look at me, *I'm* afraid. Even if I see something going on wrong, I'm afraid to say because you can't trust the Police Department.

Young Negroes and Puerto Ricans seem to react more violently to the police than their elders. Teen-agers spend more time in the streets and, even when innocent, are irritated by police who chase them from the corner, question them when school windows are broken, rebuke them when a street water hydrant is opened, or become otherwise involved in teen-age pranks. Incidents that go unnoticed in middle class white areas are conspicuous in Harlem where as many teen-agers may live in a single block as live in many white suburbs. One teen-age Negro boy expressed a common sentiment:

They beat up on kids for nothing, you know, shoot them and that. Then bring up excuses that they were going to come up with a knife. They're Negro or they're Spanish, that's mostly it. Those cops should get it through the head that they're no better than Negroes or Puerto Ricans.

Girls and women have had fewer encounters with the police, but many have seen or heard things. One thirteen-year-old Puerto Rican girl thought whites—the police in particular—had something to learn from the Puerto Rican people:

The police should be more friendlier now. They're killing people. I think some of them are frightened, and they're not thinking of what they're doing. They shouldn't kill. They should injure them better—or try to find out why they're doing these things—and try to be more civilized. The white people should be friendlier with the colored people. Cause there's nothing really wrong with them. Right now where I live there's a lot of Negroes there. We all get along together. A lot of white people—and we get along. We do it, why can't other people do it? It's the same thing.

It is because, in East Harlem, people *do* live side by side and they *do* "get along," better than in most places, that rioting did not erupt there.

A Negro woman offered a helpful suggestion:

I haven't seen any brutality myself. The policeman should be *known* in the neighborhood, and I think special police should be assigned to each neighborhood, so the people will get to know *him*, and *he* will get to know the people. He will see just how the people in the community go about each day. The people shouldn't be afraid of the policeman. I think he's there for their protection. That way the teen-agers will become less afraid of the police—if the police become friendly and can advise them right and wrong. They should have a heart-to-heart talk, and that way the boys who have no fathers in the home would have someone to talk to. If the police understood, they could help the boys understand, and *they* would know how the white man felt about it.

Some fifth grade children offered these comments on police behavior:

—When the cops come the people throw bottles out the windows at the cops.

—I seen people gamble, and I seen the police gamble, too. On our block people play numbers. If I was one of those ladies that saw a policeman doing something, I would call the chief and tell him. The bookies? They run around like clowns. They do. Every night you see it. These guys every night they go into the basement. One night a cop went down there. Every day in my block, you know, they gamble.

—You know there was this man sleeping over there, and the policeman came and took out a blackjack and hit him and said, "Get up," and the man said, "Just a minute" he didn't have his shoes on, so he was going to put on his shoes. And when he said like that, the policeman hit him. He took out his blackjack and smacked him. He turned him over and put handcuffs on him. And the bum didn't do nothing. He didn't say nothing to the cop. They're just crazy, man.

—They see you walking down the street. They think you're going to do something bad, so they rap the stick on you, because the police watch the Negroes so they could swing at them good. They don't have no right. You know I don't find nothing different between colored people and the white people. I think they should have the same rights we do.

A Negro woman spoke from some personal experience with police:

I really don't think most police are brutal, because my husband is a policeman. I've seen chicken police. . . . "Let me make friends with those in the neighborhood in case something happen." . . . Then, "I'm not *here* buddy. I'm going to *hide*." You know, I've seen that. And I've also seen where something is happening, they'll go and hide for half an hour. They come out, "Well, what's the big deal?" you know. And then you've got good officers. And then you've got the hard officer. I think he does all this. Sometime he's a little too hard. I've never seen any brutality.

Many people, including a middle-aged Negro woman, believed that the police got no cooperation in the neighborhood and that this aggravated the crime problem. Unlike some others, this woman did not find any scarcity of police.

This community is crawling with policemen. But let me tell you something. The people here *harbor* a criminal—because if it's *your* son you're going to protect your son. You protect your son because he's yours and you love him. But don't hide him in his wrongdoing. If my son has committed a robbery and hurt somebody in the process, he has to go: "I'm with you 400 per cent, I'm fighting for you, but what you did was wrong." But, oh no, everybody says it wasn't their son, it was somebody else's. It wasn't my husband or boy friend or whoever it is, you know.

Like most others, a young Puerto Rican man had both good and bad experiences with police:

Some of the police are bad, and some are very good. They got a job to do. The ones I have seen in this neighborhood are very good. I could be out here at four o'clock in the morning, coming home from work, and they see me and say, "Hello, is everything all right? Well, we'll watch you, we'll watch you from here." But some are very nasty: "Where's your identification?"—you know. Right away they get snotty with you, and you've got to shut your mouth. If he's asking you for a certain reason, he should ask you in a proper way and not try to get smart with you.

An eloquent and angry Negro man was obviously not an extremist or a Black Nationalist, but his sentiments, like those of many Negroes, were strong and heated:

I think the situation right now is going to be as bad, if not worse, than the situation was in Germany with the Germans and the Jews.

This is my personal opinion. I would expect them any minute to start building furnaces. People laugh, but to me I don't think that it's that funny. They laughed. The Berlin Jews said the same thing, that Hitler wouldn't go this far, until they found themselves, the same Jews, marching, and being put into these furnaces. It doesn't look that way NOW. But with people like Goldwater and the reactionaries, and with the country swinging toward the right, the John Birch society, the Ku Klux Klanners, and with these Irish cops and the Negro hater per se, I think the thing is swinging that way. Because the Negro is tired of being in the position he is in and has been in for the last four or five hundred years. The darker race all over the world is on the march, and this man [the white man] knows it. He knows [that] his defeat and his being put into place, so to speak, is inevitable. He knows this. And he is doing everything he possibly can to keep the darker races from progressing. This is my personal opinion.

It's not just here, it's all over America. This tension. This man sees his daughter in bed with a black boy. And this thing hurts him more than anything else. He wakes up screaming. I don't mean literally, I mean figuratively. And this is the one thing that's worrying him more than anything else. He don't want this to happen. He sees all the dirt that he has done towards the dark races of the entire earth, maybe being brought back to him. All his crimes that he has committed, being brought back to him, and he's afraid of this. That's all it is. The man is living in fear. I went up to Harlem the other night, to 121st Street, and I saw a policeman. These were scared people, man. These were panicky people. The police—yes—panicky!

There's a solution to it. The walls of the ghetto have to be let down. You can't keep people confined in a ghetto and expect to have peace. For example, we have this school situation with the pairing off and the busing. This is ridiculous for people to even question something like this. The problem is not in busing the children. The problem is that you and I, practically, cannot live where we want to. In other words if I can live where I want to, where I, as a human being, could afford to, without any burning crosses and disturbances in my backyard and all that crap, then there would be no problem about what school my children go to.

They go to school in the required neighborhood. The problem is not the pairing. You see, it's like you got a pimple on your face, man, and you treat the pimple rather than treat the cause on the inside. And we're trying to shift this whole weight on the children. Even their *own* children is bearing the brunt of their stupidity, their hatred, and their ignorance. You understand? And their fear. That's my opinion. Harlem is a ghetto, like the wall in Germany, and this man is keeping us jammed up in here.

The only solution is to let people live where they're supposed to live or where they can afford to live and where they want to, regardless of whether they're black or white. This is the problem. The problem is not that police are brutal or this and that. You should see one of these blocks on a hot summer day. Rats and roaches. Living like pigs and animals. They *got* to come out in the street, and when they come out in the street they're all on top of each other. They can't *stand* each other, really. That's the whole problem. They hate each others guts in a sense. Not that they hate each other, it's just that they get on each others nerves. If I was all day—making noise and singing, throwing bear cans and bottles, kids running all over your feet—you can't sit down and relax like a human being and enjoy a cool drink and some music—like the colonels down south with those mint juleps. I mean, man, let's face it, that's no way for a human being to live.

The real criminals in the slum are not the poor. They are more nearly the victims of crime. Perhaps the most heinous of slum crimes is the sale of heroin. In 1962 two brothers were picked up in East Harlem for possession and sale of massive quantities of heroin. One was taking orders in his clothing and toy store; the other delivered it in his taxi. Both were white. After a five-year study in Philadelphia, Dr. Marvin E. Wolfgang, sociologist at the University of Pennsylvania, concludes that Negroes were victims of white offenders "approximately three times more frequently than were whites victims of Negro offenders."

In general in the slum, and in the city, more people seem to be concerned about crime than about police brutality, though both are sources of anger and fear. In a poll conducted among Negro residents of Central Harlem and Bedford-Stuyvesant (Brooklyn) by the *New York Times*, the question was asked: "There has been a lot of talk lately about police brutality. As far as you know, is there a lot of police brutality, is there only a little, or isn't there really any police brutality at all?" Twelve per cent answered, "A lot," 31 per cent, "A little"; 20 per cent, "Not at all"; 34 per cent, "Not sure"; 3 per cent, no answer.

The most startling responses came in answer to the question: "What would you say is the biggest problem that Negroes here in this part of the city have to worry about?" Crime was rated the "biggest problem" by more people than education. It was given third place and education fourth.

FEAR

Many slum dwellers live in a generalized state of fear—of being robbed, knifed, attacked, bullied, or having their children injured. The fear colors their whole lives: their ability to learn, to work, to stay sane and healthy, to venture out of their apartments or block, to live openly and freely, to be friends with their neighbors, to trust the world, outsiders, themselves. Fear is a crippler in the slum.

In East Harlem, with its vast youth population, only 10 per cent of the nonstreet acreage is park. So children play in the streets. In Morningside Manhattan, a neighboring area with more money and fewer children, 37 per cent of the acreage is park. In East Harlem, the streets take up almost half of all acreage; it is here that children play and the business of life is carried on. Cars have more room than children.

In New York most people who get enough money to do it move out. They move to the edge of town or to the suburbs or farther. Many of them prefer the excitement of the city and hate long-distance commuting, but they do it "for the sake of the children"—good schools, open space, safety from crime, housing space for big families. Most of the people in East Harlem who live in bad housing are either too poor to move out or don't know where to go. They remain with their children.

East Harlem's children seem afraid. Almost all of them have witnessed crime or violence in the neighborhood or at school, and they are afraid. The children complain about the older boys from higher grades and from the junior high schools who hang around the school and bully them:

Some boys come from junior highs to the halls, and they carry knives, and they say to the little boys, "Give me your money or we'll cut you up and all that."

Five years ago when this school was uncivilized, you know, it was real bad, and this kid he came to school, and he was crazy, he was drunk, you know, and he was big and he had a knife, and he said he was going to cut Mr. A——'s hair. So I ran. I was scared, and I went to tell, but where were all the teachers at? And I hear the teachers screaming out loud, and they were all locked up in there.

Many children complained about the bad men and bad children and about the things they "learn" in the streets. One child said:

There's too much bad men. I say everywhere is a bad neighborhood. Not like around here but everywhere you go you could see a bad one. On the west side on a hundred fifth, in Brooklyn, where my grandmother lives, it's real quiet. You walk in there, and you could hear a pin drop. At 7 o'clock everybody's in their house, and nobody's in the street. That's better than around here, 'cause nobody disturbs you. This neighborhood is worse than other places. Too much big people teach the little kids too much bad things. The boys take the pocketbooks and pass it to each other. Too much people got too much bad ideas. The little kids learned it from the big ones. The little kids can be worse as the big kids. As they grow up they get worse.

Though the youth "gangs" are mainly gone from East Harlem, the "clubs" remain and sometimes their activities are indistinguishable from those of the fighting gangs.*

And they report much worse things than gambling, things they have witnessed themselves or that happened to relatives or neighbors:

—The neighborhood is lousy. Like if the people, say, rap on your door, and they bust in the door, they steal from you. And yesterday right in front of everybody, a man shot a man in the back with a 35. Shot him in the back.

—There was this little biddy, she went down to 100th and First Avenue, and came back and met these boys at 111th Street and they took her up to apartment, and they beat her up bad and her face was swollen, and they gave her an injection, an overdose of narcotics. They all took narcotics. And then she dies. And they find her in bed dead in the apartment.

—Every Sunday my mother goes to see my brother at the state hospital, and she takes his things, and I help her because, you know, her hands they hurt, and this finger she had a big bumps on it. So every Sunday I take her things to the bus, and when coming back, there was this man, he was standing next to the stoop, and these other two men came out and shot at him. He put that thing on so you couldn't hear the shot, and he killed the man, and then they went away, and I was there when everything happen. Some people are killing other people for nothing, they're taking away their lives.

Parents are often so afraid of the street and the strange things that happen there that many of them keep small children at home, summer and winter. Discussions with children show that knowledge and fear of crime, fights, abuse from other children, are at the top of their minds. Children talk about it so much and so freely that it seems almost a preoccupation. Fear can be

* Despite recent substitution of narcotics for knives among fighting gangs, delinquency is more than twice the city rate. Among the remaining youth clubs are: Red Wings, Viceroys, Dragons, Enchanters, Enforcers, Elegants, Untouchables.

so damaging to the human personality and to learning potential that those who inquire into the causes of limited growth among slum children had better look at the streets as well as the home and the school.

Few people outside the law enforcement agencies deal with crime directly, and no one has tried to test the dimensions of fear in the slum.

Preston Wilcox, a Negro social worker, said, "One reason crime is rampant in East Harlem is that Negroes won't turn other Negroes in to a white policeman. Whites just don't know the type of treatment Negroes get from the police." The same is said to apply to Puerto Ricans. If this is the case, some means should be devised of allowing local citizens to help enforce the law. Wilcox also suggested that "instead of adding more police —nobody thinks that will do any good—they should sit around with people and ask what they can do to make their houses safer. That's the only way to do anything about it. One person suggested sealing off the roofs; that's where the thugs and addicts hang out, and there's no reason to leave them open anyhow. People have a lot of good ideas."

Again, the familiar theme: The people of East Harlem need to take power and exert controls over their own destiny.

The three keys to American democracy are involvement, civic spirit, and volunteerism.
—ALEXIS DE TOCQUEVILLE

8 | Organizing Self-help and Protest: Community Organization, Development, and Mobilization

Social workers, ministers, and new militants seem to agree on at least one thing: The people of East Harlem need to be organized. They disagree on the organizing formula, however, and split their views over whom to organize, how to organize, and the purposes of organizing. The three familiar approaches to community progress—community organization, community development, and community mobilization—represent some of the divergent views.

Most communities in the industrialized world are honeycombed with voluntary and informal associations, organizations of people with similar interests for mutual aid. In general the richer and older the area, the more organizations there are to join and meetings to attend. Though the poor chat together informally as much as anyone, they rarely go to meetings. Their counterparts in the white collar middle class spend much of their lives in meetings and participation in organizations. Usually their business and their personal lives are hooked in securely to organization charts. Many organization men do almost nothing, professionally, but organize. The meeting, large or small, is the symbol of that organization life, a life that offers orderly channels and opportunities to move up in the world.

The poor man is short on formal organizational skills. He is inexperienced at getting people to participate, setting up an agenda, leading a meeting, establishing committees, working out agreements, delegating authority, articulating his views, speaking up, raising a point of order, or passing a motion. He is usually not very good at meeting people or making them feel welcome at meetings. He is usually retiring about talking to strangers or making new friends. These underdeveloped social skills may handicap him as much as his shortage of job skills.

Among poor migrant groups, the most successful seem to have been the most highly organized. Similarly the more successful *individuals* have often been those with the best sense of organization. The rapid adaptation of Jewish immigrants to the New World, for example, may be as closely linked to organizational skills, developed within the community, as to a history of urban living and other factors.

In the urban slum the "underworld" can often take over and run things. It may be the only effective organization present; it moves into a vacuum.

Though "neighborhood improvement" block clubs in Detroit and elsewhere have given the poor new strength and responsibility, in East Harlem the block organization has not dug in. People are not in touch with each other, and they seem to live more in fear than friendship. In other communities, outside New York, political clubs have set up solid organizations among low income people; unions have organized them as workers, and various agencies have organized them as residents. Relatively few of East Harlem's poor take part in such organizations. Most of the old immigrants have moved out, and their political machines have folded. These machines, even when they got kickbacks, offered the poor some real power and access to funds and public policy. In East Harlem the old immigrant political clubs (Tammany and others) for all their flaws and rude manners helped the immigrant poor get on their feet. They organized the political districts block by block, precinct by precinct. They knew people by name, and they provided services, referrals, advice, and assistance. Now the old Italian machine in East Harlem is out of order, at least temporarily, and there is not yet a good substitute for the new Puerto Rican and Negro voters.

Preston Wilcox was my excuse for going to East Harlem in the first place. I went there to discuss with him his self-help approach to social work and his ideas about community organization. It was a longer discussion than I expected.

Wilcox, an unorthodox Negro social worker, joined the faculty of the Columbia University School of Social Work, but his main laboratory is still East Harlem. There he has given for more than five years a practical demonstration of his ideas as director of the East Harlem Project, a community self-help project sponsored by Union and Johnson settlements. On his new job he trains students in community organization including Peace Corps work.

Wilcox says the people themselves, the "Little Joes" of East Harlem and other places, will have to design the plans for their communities, make the decisions, lay the bricks; or the new structure which is put up after the old one is cracked by street demonstrations will be just as rotten as the old one. His approach may suggest the shape of this rebuilding when the street parades thin out, as they have, and the hard work begins.

He is not, by temperament or professional commitment, an agitator. One of the most seasoned advocates of community arousal, Saul Alinsky, of Chicago's Industrial Areas Foundation, starts with agitation. He arouses people about genuine grievances, and from their group protests come the community leaders and organization. Alinsky calls his work community mobilization to distinguish it from other forms of organization. Wilcox's approach is more subdued. Still, it goes far beyond the usual social work community organization that often organizes only among the top brass who then pull strings for people below. He wants to give everyone a chance to join.

Wilcox says of the new mass action: "The best thing that's come along. I've never seen a more creative use of conflict." Our nation, he says, "works best in a conflict situation. We've got to try to sustain the crisis." Before the election hiatus in street parades, he agreed with the lady picket and others in East Harlem who witnessed some real forward movement in the community: "We've got a great fire burning here and we don't want to put it out."

How does he go about his undefinable job? "There is a muscle-building quality," he says, "in letting people do things for themselves. To get people to participate you have to let them in on the planning. Many agencies don't want to yield control. You have to be a secure person to let Joe come through." Opportunity, respect, and responsibility: These are his favorite words. "We help people to help themselves."

Wilcox is, among other things, a dealer in meetings: arranging them, talking about them, going to them. The first morning we met, Wilcox and I talked for several hours. Around 1:30 the idea of lunch came to him, as a kind of afterthought, and we headed for a tavern down the street. People on the street nodded to him and exchanged greetings. One was the manager of the new East Harlem bank. Wilcox, proud as a major investor or a new father, took me inside this temple of finance—"the first in East Harlem in twenty-five years, and already with 13,000 depositors and $3 million on deposit, and another new bank opening down the street."

"Poor communities," he said, "are misunderstood. People don't call on their resources. One gal raises ten thousand a year for her church without trouble. Poor people are generous. If you're poor you have to learn to share because there will be times when you don't have."

In contrast to Negroes who grow up in city ghettos, Wilcox has "no energy to waste on racial bitterness; how can I be bitter when people who have given me so much are of a different race?" His attitude reflects the climate in which he grew up. In his home town, Youngstown, Ohio, there was then, no racial hostility, no building of fences. People worked together in peace, he says. His was one of only two Negro families on the block, so mainly he hung out with whites until adolescence, when things change. Son of a steel-mill laborer from Alabama who writes only his name, and a Georgia mother with a natural flair for community work, he looks back with warm nostalgia on his early family life. "My mother never took anything lying down." Apparently this buoyancy runs in the family.

Like many social workers, Wilcox seems strangely detached from politics, which he regards as corrupt, though his relations with local politicians have been cordial. This aloofness tends to remove him and the people he reaches from the hard realities of power in the city and the main avenue of hope for the poor. But it provides a kind of community neutrality that most social workers seem to feel they need.

Wilcox views with a certain skepticism the current upsurge in what is known as community organization as a remedy for the ills of the slum. In New York the Youth Board, the schools, Health Department, urban renewal, and other agencies all have a staff of community organizers. So does Mobilization for Youth in the Lower East Side. Everyone seems suddenly to be getting into the act. Each works from different premises. Some community organizers, Wilcox says, are simply "tranquilizing communities," pacifying unrest, rather than stimulating activity. Other programs which employ dozens of professionals from the universities at fine salaries, he calls adventures in "university politics," whose main effect is to give good jobs to social workers.

Sometimes an idea for action has come from citizens and sometimes from the Project staff. One Christmas it was the Project's idea to put up a Christmas tree. The staff got four trees and set up community signs around them. Several years later, dozens of trees were being put up by the citizens, fifty-three in one project alone. Because the residents put them up, the trees stay put.

"One of the major deterrents to citizen participation in an area like East Harlem is the fact that the important decisions are made by persons who have little understanding or identity with the community." School principals, housing managers, and public officials, Wilcox said, fall into this category. Citizens "become experts at resisting authority and procedural inertia— or else at yielding to it completely."

The Project staff tries to bring the citizens into conferences with "authority figures" to foster better mutual understanding. Staff has had to spend more time with the "authority figures," persuading them to listen to lay opinion, than it has with the citizens themselves, persuading the latter that their efforts to change things would not harm them.

"Local adults have had much greater impact on changing *public* policies than they have in changing the policies of *private* agencies. This is indeed a sad commentary."

With encouragement from the Project, citizens now serve on local school boards and other community committees. Some run for public office. Groups that began by using the Project office and supplies for meetings are now out on their own and have their own resources.

Leaders have been developed through workshops, educational trips (to Washington, etc.), and participation in study and action programs.

He described the new community organizers from public agencies as "company agents." Though they tend to have a "deep commitment about people" their work in "large bureaucracies causes them to become no more than company agents imposing the will of their agencies on the communities to which they are assigned. A major exception is the manner in which the Housing Authority deploys its staff to serve its tenant groups." Conflict is necessary, he thinks; "pain and change" are inescapable.

He does not like charisma or "playing one group against another." "Winning or losing doesn't matter. You don't need the community if you simply want to win. I could accomplish many of these things myself, without the community."

His own method is to listen, to let others grow to his size or beyond. And as you watch, you respect his principles and his gift. He seems one of those rare individuals whose middle class values are an asset to those who do not yet share them. As he uses them, his gifts are not patronizing, superior endowments, but simply the readily shared attributes of a friendly and helpful neighbor.

His goal for others is autonomy and self-help. The woman who straps the child tightly to the maternal apron strings makes the same error as the benefactors who control the lives of "those poor people" and will not give them room or incentive for independence and self-direction. The tradition of having things done *for* it, rather than *with* it, has robbed East Harlem of its grass roots potential, he feels.

The East Harlem Project that Wilcox has directed provided staff assistance to more than ten parent groups and eight public-housing tenant groups. A delegate body of parent leaders and tenant leaders has developed, but no other "continuing coordinating organization."

As you watch the whole process of self-help, you see that this is a slow and tortuous path to progress, though perhaps the only sound route. One bitter December night, for instance, I went to a meeting of public housing tenants. Misguided by the notice that sent me into the pool room, perambulator room, Boy Scout room, I arrived just after the meeting began, forty minutes late. I counted twenty-three in attendance, including five outsiders like myself. All the English spoken was translated into Spanish for two Puerto Rican women. One articulate tenant talked about school open house and urged parents to go and talk with teachers. A demand was being made, one elderly Negro woman said, for a new junior high school "which we sure need badly." Grievances directed at the city and the Housing Authority poured out: More street lights were needed to prevent mugging. Why should tenants have to pay when a main fuse blew? Tenants were throwing bottles around and should be stopped. The door buzzers and locks were not in order, and the outside door should be locked. One citizen said after completing a leadership course, "I used to think a leader meant Mayor Wagner or President Eisenhower, but I know now that I am a leader too."

The key role played by staff, Wilcox said, was "to behave in such a way that people felt that they were *expected* to give their utmost."

Sustaining the interest of citizens when there is no crisis is a problem. The Project has attacked this in several ways. It has helped groups develop "service functions" (clothing exchanges, teen canteens, etc.) that are missed when absent. It has helped groups obtain regular meeting places. It has made them representatives on delegate bodies where their absence would be noted. It has helped them publish regular newsletters to members about community and city affairs. All these have helped *sustain* interest and activity. Continuity is also interrupted by the personal problems of citizen leaders. "Since the leadership core is comprised essentially of women," baby-sitting, childbirth, family problems all take a heavy toll.

Significantly, turnover resulting from a change of address is minimal in East Harlem. "The greatest interruption occurs," Wilcox says, "among Italian and Puerto Rican women whose husbands tend to want them in the home in the evenings rather than chairing a P.T.A. meeting." Another source of disruption is that many of the leaders could not be reached by telephone during their work hours; so the staff usually does the "research."

What the Project found was that citizen groups started out mainly with complaints about the conduct of social agencies and ended up examining themselves and their own conduct.

The Project would like to include research in its action program, and it would like to "stimulate the local leaders to engage in a *comprehensive attack* on the problems of the crowded and changing urban center—where it previously worked on specific problems."*

When the Project began, in 1957, it operated on an *ad hoc* basis—temporary groups to deal with specific problems. There was no mass group, no permanent structure. But the staff has moved away from the *ad hoc* into organizational matters—constitutions, elections, developing leadership and *esprit de corps*—and the hope has been to launch a "comprehensive" organization.

The Project would also like to create "apprenticeships in community development." Convinced that the community needs, more than anything, to develop its own skills and leaders —rather than being spoken for by professionals—the Project wants to set up a "leadership training and guidance program" for about seventy-five men and women a year, to be paid $1.25 per hour for attending "special skill, practice and information sessions." For about forty weeks, they would train four hours a week, while at the same time taking part in unpaid community action. It is one variation on a new and popular theme: the use of "indigenous people" in paid community work.

> *All the people arose as one man.*
> —JUDGES

The "mobilization" approach to community organization is quite different. Saul Alinsky is its leading exponent. Alinsky, former University of Chicago criminologist, has been organizing communities since the mid 1930s. He doesn't like the "nice-

* "Operation: Community Redevelopment," Draft proposal, September 26, 1962.

nelly" social work connotations of "community organization," preferring instead "mass mobilization." "The social workers' success at sustaining purposeful involvement of lower income peoples," he said, "is conspicuously absent." For these words and others, he is said to be *persona non grata* with social workers. His only work in New York City has been in the Chelsea area, where the community was split open on the urban renewal issue, with a Catholic priest leading Alinsky's antirenewal fight, which was lost.

Founded twenty-four years ago, his Industrial Areas Foundation received large donations from industrialists, merchants, labor leaders, and the Roman Catholic and Presbyterian churches. More recently his major source of revenue seems to be the Catholic church.

The problem is that the underprivileged have no power over their lives and they know it. They want bread and opportunity; instead they're offered consolation, adjustment, arts and crafts, fun and games. No wonder they fail to respond. That's like prescribing aspirin to cure cancer. Show them how to get the power to achieve what *they* want, not what somebody else thinks is sufficient for them, and they'll uplift their community themselves.

Alinsky uses the tactics of politics and unionism and thinks of himself as an agitator. His usual approach is to make peace with some of the power groups in these areas—the Catholic church, political parties, and local unions—and let them subdue the opposition that is usually stirred up. Giving people power does not insure they will *use* it properly. But they cannot use it properly, of course, if they don't *have* it.

His biggest problem is finding organizers. He wants "people who can burn against injustice with a hot anger, but who can bridle their anger so that it becomes cold and hard. This way they can act with calculation." When an organizer goes on the job, he starts by walking the streets, ringing doorbells, talking to whoever opens the door. He listens and tries to find out what's bothering people, what issues can "unite them in anger."

Claims about human rehabilitation are impressive. One I.A.F. organizer says: "I don't know how many houses have been rehabilitated but I can tell you about individuals, how they've changed. Once they were fearful, scared, hesitant. It was impossible to do anything. The people were apathetic, without hope. Then all of a sudden they were not afraid, not fearful. By God, they say, we *can* whip the enemy."

Sometimes the organizers let people make their own mistakes, because they are "more concerned with teaching people than winning any particular issue."

In some New York communities (the Lower East Side, Central and East Harlem) recurring efforts have been made to bring in the I.A.F. to organize.

Some people in East Harlem dismiss "agitation" as an organizing device. "Anyone can agitate people and whip them up, that's easy—but it doesn't last." We have to build understanding and "lasting organizations," they say. On the other side it is said that you cannot organize the impoverished *except* through agitation, and that the only lasting organizations of low income people are labor unions, which were organized through agitation. I.A.F. organizations also have notable longevity.

"Conflict" is the issue that separates the mobilizers from some of the organizers. The mobilizers believe that sharp conflict between the powerful and the powerless is necessary and inevitable, that the powerless cannot be organized except to fight the enemy or the system. On the other side, the "soft" organizers think conflict is bad and divisive and that people should be taught to work together and cooperate. The mobilizers, in rebuttal, say that the best way to get people together is through conflict and struggle. One side in this argument wants to resolve social conflict, the other to resolve it by stimulating it first.

Alinsky's Temporary Woodlawn Organization (TWO), in a Negro area near the University of Chicago, is a federation of some 85 community groups, including 13 churches, 3 business associations, and other local groups. It is said to represent some

30,000 people, and 1,200 attended the second annual convention in 1963. Alinsky insists that his mobilizations have a full-time paid staff. TWO began with demonstrations and an action program over merchant chiselers, an issue that both local "reputable" businessmen and consumers are concerned about. It moved into rent strikes and other issues. TWO, like other mobilization projects, hopes to become permanent, independent of the I.A.F. staff, and self-supporting. Its independence is running behind schedule.

"TWO's greatest contribution," says Charles Silberman, "is its most subtle: it gives Woodlawn residents the sense of dignity that makes it possible for them to accept help."*

Success in organizing obviously depends on the skills of the organizers. These skills can be learned if organizers have natural aptitudes. The I.A.F. selects people with proven ability and, through training sessions, sharpens their skills. Very little is written about organizing techniques. A significant as well as a fascinating subject, it needs much fuller exploration.

THE RURAL SCENE AND PUERTO RICO'S COMMUNITY EDUCATION

The East Harlem Project is close to and in the debt of Puerto Rico's Community Education program, whose work is worth reviewing. In Puerto Rico, work in the community does not mean mobilization, it means education. It is community development with a Puerto Rican accent.

Fred Wale, Puerto Rico's Community Education director, says that the project's purpose is education to help people examine and question the conditions of their lives. Its purpose is not economic development but human development. "Our culture is a dependent, anthoritarian one . . . because of our rural settlements" and so the goal is to get people to live consciously, not submissively.

* Charles Silberman, *Crisis in Black and White,* New York: Random House, 1964, p. 348.

The project works in some four hundred rural communities. An "educator"—a man with human understanding—is assigned to work with eight communities. The educator is often a person without professional training, who can "identify" with the villagers. The *campesinos* usually meet outdoors with the educator, and together they watch films, read books aloud, and discuss for some twelve weeks.

The books, films, graphic arts all go together and are of exceptional quality. The booklet, *Los Derechos del Hombre*, deals with man's struggle for his rights. Another book deals with timidity: "The community is full of men and women with dignity and courage who have remained silent on many matters having to do with their communal living . . ." One book tells the story of two mice, Ignacio, "who accepted what life brought him" and Santiago, who "learned that he was more man than mouse." The book *Las Ideas, los otros y you* deals with intolerance. "People who live fully, richly, proudly can live in close physical relationship and still be tolerant of each other. Self-respect and love of one's neighbor dispel the doubts and darkness upon which fear, jealousy and envy breed."

Then the people talk about their problems and what they would like to do. When the community reaches a consensus then they search for the help they need. "They visit the local offices of the agency involved; health, agriculture, sanitation, water, education. They talk to the mayor. They go to San Juan. And always in a spirit of learning not of demanding." They ask the technicians to come to their meetings. The people build roads, schools, wells, community centers, and the government contributes about half the cost.

"The technician who visits a so-called isolated community and thinks only of latrines or diarrhea sees his problem through the small end of the telescope. On the other hand, if he goes with the belief that spiritual isolation is a hundred times more deplorable than physical, his perspective will take on the dimensions of truth. In this respect all of us can become one as we enter the community and sit with respect and love in the circle of continual development."*

That is one form of community development. It is educational, not economic development.

YOUTH

> *There is a heritage of noble obligation which young*
> *people accept and long to perpetuate. The desire for action,*
> *the wish to right wrong and alleviate suffering, haunts*
> *them daily. They hear constantly of the great social mal-*
> *adjustment, but no way is provided for them to change*
> *it, and their uselessness hangs about them heavily.*
>
> —JANE ADDAMS

Bridges are always a strategic target. Manhattan, an island, is fed by its bridges. To tie them up is to tie up business activity in the city, if not the nation and the world. In early 1964 a new East Harlem chapter of CORE issued this statement as seven of its members lay down on the Triborough Bridge and backed up traffic for twenty minutes.

East River CORE is engaging in civil disobedience today to protest the unsafe and overcrowded schools in East Harlem.

We regret to inconvenience people passing through our neighborhood on their way home to the better sections of the city, but we are both very sorry and very angry about the way that Negro and Puerto Rican children are treated in the richest city in the wealthiest country in the world. We ask commuters to look more closely at the schools in our community because they are so unlike many of the schools in Queens and Long Island.

A number of our schools, built back in 1883, are potential fire traps. P.S. 80 had a fire last Sunday in a room next to the gymnasium. If it had occurred during the school day and spread to the rest of the building many children would have died. The debris from this fire has still not been cleaned up.

---

* Fred Wale, "A Program of Community Development," *Health Educators at Work*, Chapel Hill, University of North Carolina, 1961.

East River CORE works in a community where the schools are immensely overcrowded. Schools built to hold 500 children now hold over 1,000. Many have no auditoriums, few toilets, cracked plaster and overcrowded lunchrooms. When the children eat, they smell the garbage close by.

We are asking that New York commuters stop for a moment to look at Harlem and the people they leave behind, and that they do something about this problem, that is not only Harlem's, but all America's.

The "East River Rats" came out with the rent strike and began organizing in the Triangle. The Rats were a proudly self-named CORE group composed of Negro and white youths who broke away from the older CORE chapter in Harlem to try out some new ideas about neighborhood organization. They wanted to build a base in the black community.

They set up an office in Melvin Schoonover's Baptist church and after a few weeks numbered some 54 members, with another 100 supporters close by. Few of them live in East Harlem. In the first few weeks of work, they put two buildings on rent strike, tied up the Triborough, arranged a truce between two rival gangs, started a basketball team for youths, exposed the problems of the Triangle's schools, went door to door in the neighborhood, arranged some tutoring, and talked about setting up a secretarial school.

They came to the Triangle with a plan they had been working on for eighteen months. The group divided into five teams —three to organize in assigned blocks, one to work on the rent strikes that come out of the organization, and the fifth to take on the schools. They defined the problems ahead of time— housing and schools—but were anxious to hear about other problems.

The teams found out within forty-eight hours what was going on in the blocks assigned. Before they knocked on any door, they scouted. They talked to merchants, went into the bars, the barber shops, beauty parlors, club houses, whatever was around. They wanted to find out what illegal activities were going on so that they could step around them.

After the trouble-makers were known, the youths began to knock on doors. Charlie Saunders, eighteen-year-old high school student who has "organized his high school solid," says with a look of wide-eyed innocence, "If we keep this up, pretty soon we'll have the whole city organized." He is the leader of the school team and now knows as much as the experts about the Triangle schools.

Some CORE groups are "afraid of the guys downstairs—from the streets, the poolrooms, the gangs, the reform schools," one member says. "We are not. We are from the streets."

The group also joined the Fifth Avenue traffic light demonstration, sponsored by an East Harlem P.T.A. In pursuit of a school crossing light, the parents tied up Fifth Avenue traffic intermittently for three days. Their placards said, "Harlem parents want lights not fights." They got the light.

"Trivia," some CORE members say. "The place is burning down and they're fiddling around with traffic lights." These critics want to join the big issues on a big scale, right away. The River Rats say that CORE needs a black base and that the only way to get it is through block organization. CORE's support has come mainly from a rather apolitical white middle class. As whites withdraw support from groups that "go too far"—and as demonstrations, without ghetto support, become more difficult—reaching the "black mass" becomes an organizational necessity. Whether such a voluntary part-time group as the River Rats (many of them students or employed elsewhere) can manage and sustain such a big job is problematic. After a few months the group splintered and moved its offices, but the main CORE continued.

The student and youth movement is organizing in the ghetto. Groups are springing up everywhere. CORE, Students for a

Democratic Society, the Northern Students Movement, and others met in mid-1964 to talk about community organizing for economic issues. Job rights rather than merely civil rights was the topic, a major shift in targets.

COMMUNITY CATALYSTS

The catalyst who apparently precipitated the East Harlem Project was Ellen Lurie. Mrs. Lurie was a volunteer with no training in social work. A Detroiter and New York University graduate, she had once heard Clarence Senior talk about Puerto Ricans, became interested in an Americans for Democratic Action project in East Harlem, and stayed there for ten years.

In 1955 the city's Youth Board did some community development work. It issued a call to all communities in the city to gather civic groups together and talk over neighborhood problems. A Town Hall study was set up in East Harlem, but it wasn't enough. After the problems were posed, the community studied, and the civic groups assembled, some action seemed in order.

Union and Johnson settlements obtained a small foundation grant and launched the East Harlem Project, employing at first both Ellen Lurie and Preston Wilcox. The two settlements worked well together because their concern for the community was greater than their institutional ego. Bill Kirk, head worker of Union Settlement, preferred the initial *ad hoc* style of organizing permanent groups. When the schools committee favored a constitution, he suggested that the small groups most involved should lead, rather than a centrally constituted body.

Top priority was the schools. The only thing to do, Mrs. Lurie said, was to get together and yell, to the right people and in the right way. But there were few voices, and those weak and discouraged. Only one school had a parent's association. A small active chorus was found in each school, and pooling them produced about sixty members of the East Harlem Schools Committee. After this August parent group studied needs in *all* East Harlem schools, they rallied, protested, and testified at City Hall —wearing big red badges saying "East Harlem." The school board, stunned by the sudden shouting from the grave, gave them new schools.

The Project began tenant organization in earnest after an attempted rape of a Puerto Rican child in 1957. The tenant drive began with Christmas. The Project staff put up a decorated tree and held outdoor group sings around it, hoping to bring people together. Within a week, the tree was stolen and the lights all pulled apart. The next year the tenants put up trees, and they stayed put.

"We never set a rigid pattern for tenants and parents associations," says Mrs. Lurie. "If someone came up with a problem, we never said 'no,' that's not our function. People came to know that they could bring up anything with us. We were constantly listening, testing out ideas. If it didn't sink—if it swam—we knew it was good—trips to Washington, summer recreation, whatever happened to grow."

Mildred Zucker, the able, lively, and devoted director of the Johnson Community Center, says: "There were no steps, we had to feel our way; no individual problem was ever left unanswered. Things open up when you have contact with people, knock on doors, talk face to face."

The Project did not always follow the community, Mrs. Lurie has said, "but it always listened and took the community into consideration." Lawn concerts were held because the professionals wanted them. Mildred Zucker wanted esthetics in Franklin Plaza and thought the community needed it. Bill Kirk was interested in consumer programs. So they did it.

In response to the criticism that the Project worked too closely with the old-line Italian political leadership, Mrs. Lurie says: "The idea in East Harlem was to look for the strong steps as well as the cracks, and build on the strong parts." The Italian leaders were there, so they worked with them.

The bulldozer produced 60,000 "strangers rattling around 13 hygienic developments—lonely, rootless, apathetic and hostile." The Project set out to make neighbors out of these strangers. "Any remedy had to start from the ground up," with lay citizens. Some of the steps taken include:

—Bringing higher income families into the community.

—Integrating Jefferson Houses: The Project organized local groups to seek out white families to integrate this project.

—Organizing tenant groups: The Project keeps activity alive with coffee hours, fish fries, building parties, tenant newspapers, and guidance.

—Strengthening the schools: Reaching the schools was difficult because it meant "winning the faith of principals and teachers, persuading them that the goal was not interference but cooperation." New PTA's have been set up in at least nine schools "including one where the principal originally resisted any such organization at all."

—Starting a school savings bank program: Because there were no banks in East Harlem, the Project set up savings banks at two schools, with over five hundred accounts opened by the children.

—Paving the way for school integration: The Project played a leading role in smoothing the way for the transfer of students from East Harlem schools to schools in white Yorkville.

—Helping teen-agers find jobs: The Project was a prime force in pushing YES (Youth Employment Service), the forerunner of many new youth job placement programs, and the Project contributes staff and leadership to the program.

—Encouraging reliable merchants: The Project has helped two groups of local merchants develop business associations. It has helped get architectural designs and win the city's support for a market that may develop into a tourist attraction.

—Strengthening the East Harlem Council: The East Harlem Council for Community Planning was set up long ago by local

groups, but it was weakened through the years by time, turnover, and the fact that many of the city employees on the
council were hesitant to take on the city. The council office
and staff were moved to the Project (both of them are now
located in Union Settlement), and the Project has helped to
revitalize this group.

—Contributing to New York City's program for East Harlem: The Project has been a liaison between the city and the
community. To succeed, the city's programs need the community's support and understanding. The Project has helped
provide this through meetings, newsletters, talks with neighbors.

—Taking the "absentee" out of absentee decisions: The Project has helped people make their own decisions and take on
responsibility. Now the city budget hearings get a strong East
Harlem delegation. Residents speak up and are heard at City
Planning Commission, Board of Education, local school board
meetings, and their political representatives are held accountable.

—Sponsoring registration campaigns: The Project has brought
together various community groups to work on voter registration. It has sponsored literacy test centers, a mobile truck unit
containing nonpartisan literature, and a sample voting machine.

—Serving as a community "clearing house": In an area of
conflicting interests, the Project often serves as "honest broker"
to mediate disputes, identify problems, and act on them. For
example, when the Board of Estimate threatened to close Benjamin Franklin High School as "underused," the Project formed a
study group to recommend action. The school stayed open.

Before the area's population changed, Union Settlement
worked mainly with youths, as most settlements do. When the
new groups came in, "most opportunity was offered in the adult
group," said Bill Kirk. They turned to adults, trying to set up
ways for people to find one another. The Project has always
operated on a shoestring—a staff of two or three, supplemented
by volunteers and the staffs of the two settlements.

Ellen Lurie left East Harlem with doubts about whether the community should fight the city so hard on renewal. "The projects have to go someplace and the slums have to come down," she said. She was not sure about the ultimate authority of lay citizens: "Where does city leadership start and community leadership stop?" The city, she felt, has some rights and duties, too. "The worst part of it is the emotion and pressure. City leaders listen and they are immobilized."

The Project has had a long list of credits. It has played a very special role. It did not set out to "mobilize" the community, but to bring people together and develop leaders, which to some extent it did. It chose to fight the city over renewal. In East Harlem, a better target might have been the slumlord.

The techniques of community organization, development, and mobilization—though significant for social change—have been hidden behind the dearth and dullness of writings that describe the process. Only the mobilizers write with strength and clarity about their work and ideas, and they are few. The literature on community organization, having enjoyed cyclical vogues among social workers for many years, has been more abundant and fatiguing. Community development, a newer process, has had relatively fewer, but choicer, words written about it.

Differences among the three are not always clear. Community organization is a social work term. It can mean many things, but it always involves getting people—at high, middle, or low levels —together for the purpose of discussing common problems. Mobilization also organizes at various levels, but organizing "the masses" is stressed, and agitation is the means of arousal.

Community development was originated on a national scale by the British to help their colonies prepare for self-government and was first called "mass education." It has been applied mainly to rural communities in developing nations. Its method is simple. It calls villagers together and encourages them to discuss and solve their own problems. Then it supplies technical and other aid when requested.

As defined by the International Conference of Social Work, community development is "the conscious process wherein small, geographically contiguous communities are assisted by the more developed, wider community to achieve improved standards of social and economic life. This is done primarily through their own local efforts and through local community participation at all stages of goal-selection, mobilization of resources, and execution of projects, thus enabling these communities to become increasingly self-reliant."

Community development tries to shake up communities that are too settled. Community organization tries to settle shaken up communities. One stirs up, the other mends. One is rural, the other urban. One is usually government sponsored, the other sponsored by private agencies. Community development produces basic change in the economic structure. It creates agricultural and industrial revolutions. Community organization is conservative. It seldom tries to produce structural change in the economy. It mends and patches and tries to help the immigrant poor make the painful adjustment to city life in a foreign country.

Community development is now being applied to cities in more than a dozen developing nations. In the United States, the federal government is encouraging local citizen participation in delinquency programs, area redevelopment, urban renewal, and programs initiated by the Children's Bureau and the Bureau of Indian Affairs. In many cities, block organizations have been set up to engage in local problem solving, sponsored by both public and private agencies.

Growing numbers of people have zealous faith in community development as a necessary (though not always sufficient) solution to poverty wherever it is found—in the city or rural community, in industrialized or in developing nations. Richard

Poston, research professor at Southern Illinois University, is among those with such faith. "Nothing that has been introduced in the current world struggle for progress," he writes, "has so typified the American pioneer tradition of work, self-help, and civic cooperation as the community development movement. And yet in all its expenditures for foreign aid the United States has given no more than token support to community development and in many cases has openly resisted it. Probably the majority of American foreign aid officials and technicians have been unaware of the concept. Many, particularly those engaged in technical assistance, have seen it as a threat to their own professional and bureaucratic interests."*

In most developing areas, he says, there is no local government, and few democratic institutions (such as informal or voluntary organizations) that would help develop "local autonomy and provide a practical vehicle for self-expression, civic initiative, and the emergence of democratic leadership." So much emphasis, he feels, has been put on physical and economic change that sight has been lost of the prime purpose of community development, "helping people to establish for themselves a participating, problem-solving society in which the chief concern is the dignity and well-being of individuals. Unless physical improvements are accomplished in this way they make little contribution toward the development of that kind of society."

Poston asserts that the only hope for the free world is to support community development, rather than indigestible technical aid, for developing areas. "All over the world American foreign aid has focused on building roads, dams, irrigation systems. . . . It has built everything but communities and democratic societies." The same situation prevails in all the developing world, he says: "The familiar ruling class, the insufferable poverty of the masses . . . and no way for people to be

---

* *Democracy Speaks Many Tongues,* New York, Harper & Row, 1962, pp. 176–177.

included in the political processes . . . or made aware of what their government is doing or of any hope to attain, peacefully, a decent standard of living in their lifetimes."

The western nations have had a democratic tradition and technical skills. They needed aid to rebuild after World War II and continue their growth. The United States gave it to them in the form of economic and technical aid. Foreign aid to *developing* nations has assumed, falsely, that the same conditions exist. In fact no political mechanism exists in the new nations, it is claimed, to digest physical aid of this type.

United States foreign aid assumed that agricultural experts and machinery would solve the problems of the new nations. "Agricultural extension in the United States represented a political system of considerable power"; it favored the "experts and machines," and it dominated ICA Point Four operations. The university agricultural extension service that worked miracles in the United States and built farm production by bringing knowledge to farmers could not produce these miracles in other areas, Poston claims. There is no "democratic system which made it possible for farmers to organize for educational purposes and to exercise a degree of initiative." The vast majority of people in the new nations were illiterate and had no tradition to "persuade them to adopt the methods of modern agriculture unless they were regimented, as in the Communist countries, or unless they were led through a type of democratic social and political development which would make it possible for them to exercise their powers of free thought, decision-making, and local initiative. They could hardly be expected to jump from the stone age to the mid-twentieth century just because a former county agent from Kansas told an official of their national government how to grow better wheat."

Community development, unlike other foreign aid programs, is coordinated and treats a community as a whole rather than as separate units that need specialized aid. When the British adopted the term in 1948, they defined it as "a movement to promote better living for the whole community with the active participation, and if possible on the initiative of the community, but if this initiative is not forthcoming spontaneously, by the use of techniques for arousing and stimulating it in order to secure its active and enthusiastic response to the movement." It is natural for professionals who have run the American foreign aid programs, Poston says, to "think not of the community in itself as constituting a problem, but rather to look upon any problem as economic, sociological, or as being in some other specialized field."

The Philippines initiated one of the first successful development programs under the late President Ramon Magsaysay after World War II. Colombia has had the most extensive program in South America. In 1952 India launched the "most gigantic effort in human history consciously to change the life conditions of a nation by democratic means." In that year Nehru launched a community development program that now extends into India's nearly 500,000 villages. A danger, warns Poston, is that the "desire for spectacular physical results may create a tendency to give up the whole idea and resort to more hasty methods." In many cases a series of "splinter projects is being pushed at the villagers," all operating in isolation of the others, and the community is not being permitted to develop its own programs.

In 1958 a three-year urban redevelopment project was launched in Delhi, India. It was a pilot project and, while it had some trouble initially, it was considered successful enough to be spread to other urban areas.* A problem is that many of the rural migrants to Delhi have no attachment to the neighborhood. In the rural village it is easier. People have families, neighbors, and they are proud of their community. The program does not

---

* "Urban Community Development, Delhi Pilot Project," Dimalananda Chatterjee, Director, Department of Urban Community Development, Municipal Corp. of Delhi, India. It may be obtained from the National Federation of Settlements, 226 West 47 Street, New York 10036.

at first attack organized crime—a major problem in Delhi—but leaves it to the organization of the people to take action.

In Gorki, in the Soviet Union, a limited community partici- pation program operates to get workers, through their unions, to help build their own homes. More than half of state-plan housing in Gorki is to be built by self-help.

In South and Southeast Asia, the Colombo Plan, begun in 1950, provides a program of technical aid from the have to the have-not nations. It has built more dams in Asia (serving three- fifths of the world's people) than any other institution, and it has provided $13,820 million in economic aid, plus much private investment. Most of the people in the area are farmers and, though agricultural production has increased about 3 per cent in the past decade in the whole region, this growth was almost completely absorbed by rising populations.

Technical aid is not enough. Perhaps community develop- ment will be more. East Harlem and the other developing neighborhoods in U.S. cities have some lessons to draw from the experiences of community development around the world.

The United States is experienced in working with rural com- munities. University agricultural extension programs have done community work in small towns and rural areas for over a cen- tury. Rural extension programs are so vast that in Michigan alone there are some five hundred county agents working for Michigan State University Extension Service as agricultural community workers. These agents organize, bring technical knowledge, develop programs. It is said that they are responsi- ble for this country's phenomenal agricultural success. Many of these agents now work in rural counties whose population has shrunk to almost nothing—while the cities, next door, bulge with people and grow unattended.

It is intriguing to speculate on the effect of one thousand urban agents (in university extension programs) working in a city like New York, which has more than twice the population of rural Michigan. If cities were served by the universities and the federal government as the rural areas have been and still are, some mortal wounds might be inflicted on urban poverty.

The universities are not without some tradition of interest in community development, aside from extension work. A description of special efforts to organize and develop small towns of the South is found in the book *Small Communities in Action* by Jean and Jess Ogden of the University of Virginia.* They conclude: "If the citizen of your community is alert to the need —if he conceives of his first job as political (in its broad sense) rather than as economic, then your community is on the way to becoming the good community."

Ernest O. Melby, while president of the University of Montana, in 1943 set up the Montana study program that reached out to small towns and encouraged groups of citizens to study the community and its needs. It got people, who had never talked together, to explore and improve their community.†

Some university programs send out consultants, on request, to aid in the solution of community problems. Daniel J. Schler of the University of Missouri, in reviewing his consulting work in sixteen communities, found that they were all small and that all requests came from the business and professional groups. In most cases the "problem" was the desire of one of these nongovernmental groups to push through a controversial program. Despite efforts to limit his contacts to the "right people," he reached out

---

* New York, Harper & Row, 1948.

† *Small Town Renaissance* by Richard W. Poston (New York, Harper & Row, 1950) is a description of Melby's work in Montana. Poston's book describes the work of the study clubs in several Montana communities, and his *Group Study Guide for Community Development* offers a manual for carrying out community studies (Division of Adult Education, University of Washington). Also see Baker Brownell, *The Human Community*, New York, Harper & Row, 1950.

A student can now major in "community organization" in some schools, including University of Missouri, Howard, Temple, Rutgers, Fordham, and the New York School of Social Work (a division of Columbia University).

to consult with "informal leaders from the unrepresented groups, primarily the poor," and to "marginal leaders who were critical of the formal leaders." Very often, he concluded, the "marginal leaders maintained a more objective view of issues and conditions" than others. To get to the level of the man on the street, the consultant has to "bore his way through the crust of formal leadership." Without this contact, the consultant often gets a "distorted view of the community." At least 75 per cent of requests had to do with creating more jobs through industrial relocation and expansion, so as to reduce emigration.

Only a few U.S. institutions of higher education have gone beyond the traditional adult education courses and into the urban slums that surround many of these tax-supported institutions. Though they continue to supply abundant aid to business and industry in the city, they have not yet extended their knowledge, skills, and technology to the city slum. The near future is likely to see these universities, aided by federal money, extending their accumulated resources to the disadvantaged. Students themselves may help initiate such programs, since they seem more concerned about community action and power than their mentors.

9

Three Local Initiatives:
The Community School,
The Study Club,
A Cooperative

The formula for slum upgrading is simple: initiative plus money. Then it gets complicated. The initiative can come from many sources, and so can the money. The best of all worlds, and the essence of democracy, is to have initiative coming from everyone—from plain citizens as well as the "leaders" and the educated who are presumably trained to take initiative. Protest is a useful tool of community arousal because it incites passive citizens to action and initiative. Tradition-incrusted agencies and institutions are also known for their passivity. But they too can and do take initiative.

This chapter is an account of three East Harlem initiatives. They deserve some detailed description because they touch two vital spots: education and housing. They are the initiatives of professionals in East Harlem, and they may be added to the list of others already described. One is the community school; the second is the study club, a supplement to the school; the third is cooperative housing, a major breakthrough into the low income ghetto. They appear here as suggestions of what might be done.

THE COMMUNITY SCHOOL

The slum school is rather like a factory. Employees punch in and out, go only out of necessity and forget it the second they are out of the door. Then the plant is empty and idle. Unlike the factory, however, the school is a *public* institution, a costly one, and its public cannot afford to let it lie idle or send its staff packing at 3 o'clock.

New slum schools, often lonely signs of affluence and promise in the ghetto, are "located" there usually only in a physical sense. They open their doors to let the children in. They close them when the children leave. The children often go out in the streets or to crowded rooms with nothing to do, no place to go.

When P.S. 108 opened, in the early 1950s, it was East Harlem's first new school in some three decades. Mary Thompson, an All Day Neighborhood School teacher, went to look over the neighborhood. What she saw was a jewel among shabby tenements. She saw a need to reach out to citizens and get them working on neighborhood problems, of which there was an extravagant excess. It was a good situation. She was in a new school, with a new and encouraging principal, and parents who were eagerly awaiting the school's opening.

Mrs. Thompson, a warm and friendly Irish woman, had never tried to organize a Puerto Rican slum. But, married to a Spaniard, she could at least speak Spanish to the neighbors.

For six months she and others spread the word that the school welcomed parents. The entire staff was "alerted to the need for extra courtesy and understanding in meeting with Puerto Ricans, who themselves are a very courteous and thoughtful people."

At the housewarming of El Barrio's new school, parents were greeted with Spanish music, piped over the public address system. Spanish was spoken that night, and all messages were translated by teachers. Parents swarmed to the school and, feeling welcome, they returned again and again. The auditorium often seated more than 450 parents at regular meetings.

Translation was a major obstacle. The staff set out to find bilingual parents. At the third parent meeting, a "man of dynamic personality helped us get the organization started." Pedro Canino, referred to then as the "mayor of East Harlem," became the first president of the parents' association.

"Through his tireless efforts," Mary Thompson said, "we got to know other parents and other citizens of the community. We also learned from him the things that would attract and keep our parents interested." Parents came to see their children honored, or to see their work or performances. They came to see Spanish films, purposely held to the end of the meeting. Coffee was served, at first American coffee; when few drank, the staff switched to Puerto Rican *con leche*. The government of Puerto Rico selected and loaned Spanish educational films. After six months, the staff felt they "had gained the confidence of the community."

Mrs. Thompson then set up a "citizens' committee." Merchants, dentists, lawyers, social workers, businessmen, and others who lived or worked in the area were called together. Again, Pedro Canino was elected chairman.

The citizens met in the school and listed community needs. At the top of the list was a summer play school. Then came adult English classes and a community center for young people.

The first project was the summer play school. Slum streets in summer are trouble spots. The school sits idle while the children lack a place for healthy recreation, and lose much of the English they learned during the school year.

The Board of Education's Division of Community Education had no funds, so the citizens set out to raise money themselves. When they came up with $1,000, collected from this impoverished neighborhood, the division agreed to open the school for the summer.

Mrs. Thompson and Adele Franklin, director of the All Day Neighborhood School, spent a month that summer without pay, trying to get the play school started. Other volunteers assisted, including teachers who gave time at the close of the school year and during their vacations. The summer play school was launched and is still afloat.

Next they tried English classes for adults. Classes were being offered at centers across the New York Central Railroad tracks, but people were afraid to pass under the railroad tunnels at night. So many adults came that the three initial classes grew to eleven. The parents who were in charge of class attendance telephoned or visited absentees to let them know they were missed and encourage them to return. Parents ran a regular June graduation for the evening English students, with party, speaker, and the usual ceremonies.

The Board of Education, accustomed to citizen action at 108, agreed to open an afterschool community center. Neighbors raised funds for needed school equipment.

Some of the members of the citizens' committee branched out into housing, sanitation, playgrounds, and other nonschool issues, and met outside the school. The Civic Orientation Center, set up by Canino, organized a rent clinic on housing problems and a sanitation squad to clean up empty lots and turn them into playgrounds. Mrs. Thompson invited them to merge into one large group working for community improvement and meet in the school.

Voter registration drives were organized. Baby-sitting services were set up. The citizens chaperoned dances. A group of kindergarten parents was formed, to meet regularly, see films, and discuss child raising and other problems. Bazaars were held to raise money, with donations from teachers and the affluent friends of ADNS. The school insisted that citizens take responsibility. If liquor bottles or narcotics were found in the building, if rules were broken, the parents and citizens dealt with the offender. Parents helped with everything. Three closets of clothes were kept in the school for children and adults. A Health Survey gave free physical examinations to over five hundred people. Disease and serious ailments of all kinds were uncovered.

Parents of course can cause awkward difficulties, and often did. Once the parents wanted a meeting on discipline. They said the teachers were hitting their kids and they didn't like it. Mrs. Thompson quite naturally put "discipline" on the agenda of the parent meeting. The school insisted that the discussion be dropped. A lopsided compromise was reached. A speaker was invited to talk about "What is discipline?", but parents were given no time to discuss their grievances.

Mary Thompson believes in the community school. She tried to get a welfare office and a health center put into the school. Welfare workers need contact with children and the school, especially in the hard-core cases, she thought, and neighbors need a close and known place to apply for relief. But the Welfare Department would have none of it. She would also like to put all community services in the school, including psychiatric and other assistance. She believes this would be better for the people and cheaper for society.

When she came to P.S. 108 there were no community services, such as she knew in New York's Chelsea section. But the resources were there: the school and neighbors. Many of the leaders she helped develop were swept away by the bulldozer, and the school had to start over with new people.

The job she did was eased by her membership in East Harlem's First Friday Club, a group of Roman Catholics with common interests, who met each month. Many "influentials" in East Harlem—doctors, lawyers, teachers, principals—came to these lunches. She always knew whom to call for help with various problems.

At least two types of school administrators work hard with parents: those who supervise the parents and those who let parents supervise themselves. The "bear hug" administrator may discourage parent independence and clamp down on expressions of protest. The "supportive" ones will encourage parents to speak up and go their own way. Mrs. Thompson always wanted the parents to take charge.

THE STUDY CLUB

Study and reading clubs have started in churches, storefronts, apartments, settlement houses, civic centers, even in school. The study club is the citizens' effort to teach basic language and learning skills to children who fall behind in school. Academic achievement is their central, and growing, concern.

One of the first clubs was born in pain. After a newspaper described one block in East Harlem as "squalid" (to which some people reacted in shock and anger) a foundation donated a storefront study club to the block. Led by a Catholic priest, a citizens' committee located the club in a store on a corner where, as it happened, a hot dog vendor was accustomed to ply his trade. By his presence, he became an adjunct watchman.*

Though some thought the club would be wrecked or used by bookmakers or narcotics pushers, discipline was not a problem on this "worst block." An average of forty-five children came and went on their own, and the club operated at capacity.

Neighbors publicized the club. "Gil Diaz, who runs a gym for fighters down the block, a Mr. Nelson, a building superintendent who seems to know everyone for blocks around were invited to the opening. They promised to tell the neighborhood about the club," said a report. Two regular volunteers showed up. Edward "Jocko" Fowler "came in soon after open-

---

* Some of these data come from *East Harlem Neighborhood Study Club*, Summary Report of the Study Club Committee, June 27, 1963, admittedly a biased source.

ing and created his own role. He chatted informally with the children, distributed supplies, jollied the curious six and seven year olds away from the entrance, and directed the puzzled to reference materials. The club lost 'Jocko' to the graveyard shift at his job. Phillip Dicker, an eighth grade student, came in to check on the stories he had heard about the club. He looked around, questioned us about our program in detail and he has been with us ever since." He comes in quietly "and almost immediately surrounds himself with two or three children whom he coaches with a professionalism that would have made Horace Mann proud."

The club's tone was warm and friendly. "Children who are too suspicious or tense to ask their teacher for help in an overcrowded classroom can work with one of the staff in an easygoing one to one relationship." Some of the children were problems in school. The club had no behavior problems. Negro, Puerto Rican, and white children all used the club. "They were waiting for us when we opened."

The original purpose of the club was to give children a place to do homework. But another problem "showed up glaringly when the children sat down to do their homework." A worker helped a child with an arithmetic problem, but "we often found that he couldn't read the statement of the problem. And when it was read to him, he was ignorant of the arithmetic operation which had to be applied for a solution."

Children were getting homework problems far beyond their reach, it was found. They did not understand basic multiplication and division and could not master simple reading. A teacher was hired to give remedial instruction.

None of the equipment has been damaged, and there is no handwriting on the walls or tables. Children who used the club were not teased or bothered by those who didn't, and there was no kidding from older children. They seemed to feel: "This is mine."

When the study club ran out of money the citizen's SOS

group (Save Our Study Club) put on a variety show to raise funds. It was a big social event in East Harlem. The hit of the show, judging by the children's response, was St. Lucy's sea cadet drill team, a mixed group (Negro, Puerto Rican, Italian) of boys from St. Lucy's Roman Catholic Church, who performed dance-like precision drill steps. The response of these normally restless children, who do not take to the usual drill, was strange. Their delight and fascination suggested that the public schools might use such "fun" drills for recreation and for instruction in discipline response.

A Twistorama, with all shapes and colors of wiggling children, a Puerto Rican band, a tumbling team, a Spanish dance, and many moaning combo singers followed. The show ended as the Freedom Singers marched up the aisle and onto the stage singing "We Shall Overcome" and carrying picket signs that said: "Equal right to know," "Truth will make us free," "Strength through study," "Knowledge is power," "Help us help ourselves," "It is our right to learn."

The study clubs flourish. Within the boundaries of P.S. 108 alone there are five. Their apparent success suggests that the neighborhood storefront, church basement, and settlement house workroom can be highly suitable places of instruction.

A COOPERATIVE

> *The people in this little settlement here seem to be very friendly. No one shuns the other. It's as though we were all the same. The children play well together. The mothers don't try to draw their children away—the white mothers don't. They've invited us to their homes—to bring the children, not to socialize really.*
>
> —A NEGRO WOMAN, FRANKLIN PLAZA RESIDENT

A recurring question is: Can middle income people be brought back to the low income ghetto?

Big bait is needed. East Harlem's first offering was Franklin

Plaza, a middle income cooperative planted deep within the ghetto.

The Plaza is as large as many good-sized towns—containing 1,635 apartments in fourteen twenty-story buildings. It is integrated: 40 per cent white, 40 per cent Negro, and 20 per cent Puerto Rican and others.* Puerto Ricans are generally poorer and not yet accustomed to project living. All apartments have light, privacy, and an open view. In the summer there are boccie courts for the Italians, play areas for the children, and a lovely promenade. Like all East Harlem developments the Plaza has large open spaces between buildings. These were put there mainly at the insistence of the settlement houses.

The Plaza converted from low to middle income during its construction. It was a way of infusing more whites and middle class people into the ghetto. Italians, uprooted by the new projects, wanted to stay in the old neighborhood but couldn't find decent housing. The city agreed to turn over the project if the neighborhood would pledge $60,000 for a cooperative. Bill Kirk, of Union Settlement and John Merli, former city councilman and local gas station owner, organized a sponsoring committee of clergymen, politicians, merchants, etc., and raised the money. About $1 million extra was put into the Plaza to make it special—stores, community recreation rooms, trees along the sidewalks, landscaping. If the Plaza had been on the margin rather than deep in the ghetto, selling would have been much easier. Strangers will put a foot inside a slum where they will not commit their lives.

Ellen Lurie and others tried to fix up the surrounding area. They pestered the Sanitation Department about the garbage pick ups, and went out to talk with the garbage team captains. They got the city to speed up the construction of a new school,

---

* It is on a ten-acre site (106 to 108 Streets, from First to Third Avenues). A three-bedroom apartment requires a down payment of $2,475, and monthly payments of $135. The rooms are rather small, especially the living rooms, but closets are ample, kitchens are large and well furnished, and everything is new.

led a campaign to get a crosstown bus for the Plaza, went to City Hall to get more street lights. A sales campaign was launched to sell the Plaza to middle class whites.

The Plaza, racially integrated (including many Chinese) is now almost sold out, and the tenant turnover is only about 3 per cent. One out of three tenants turns up at building meetings. Building parties, chess matches, bridge games, turkey raffles are held in the community center. The Plaza now has a nursery school and puts out a paper edited by Samuel Kaplan, *New York Times* reporter and tenant.

Louis Jacoby, a teacher of Spanish in the Bronx who thought it would be "romantic" to live in East Harlem, declares, "My daughter says she's never felt so comfortable in a neighborhood before. My wife says that, as far as living together with lots of different kinds of people is concerned, the place is successful. I'd say in five years' time our interests will be wider, East Harlem will have begun to pick up, and we'll have pride."

Aviva Gershweir, teacher in an East Harlem school, and her husband, a medical student, are among the Plaza's residents. The Gershweirs—young and lively—say they love living in the Plaza. Both walk to work. Their apartment is a better buy than they could find elsewhere, and they are "crazy about their neighbors." Mr. Gershweir had lived there before, in dormitory space provided by the hospital. He liked the neighborhood, and when he married he stayed on.

He was afraid at first to let his wife walk in the neighborhood, but now he feels it is as safe as any other place. He often goes to school with her, for special events, and sometimes visits Aviva's class in the afternoon. He likes the children and they like him.

Aviva walks to and from school each day. She smiles and says hello to the men and women along the way, whose faces have by now become familiar to her. "They know I'm there and who I am. They know I'm not just out on the street. The only women they bother are the ones they think are looking for something. There are no more sex psychopaths here than any-where else." She has lived at the Plaza for almost a year and has not seen or heard of anyone being bothered. "They don't bother outsiders. It's only the young men, when they have it in for someone they know."

She brings students to her apartment and visits their homes. "Sometimes I have to grit my teeth when I go in. I know some of the houses have rats, and I hate rats." Aviva grew up in a low income Italian and Negro neighborhood where hers was one of the few Jewish families, so the character of East Harlem is not unfamiliar.

Puerto Ricans are hospitable people, she says. "They welcome you to their homes so warmly when you visit. They won't let you go unless they give you something. The last family I visited gave me a little model boat; the father in the family was a carpenter and had built a twenty-seven-foot boat that he sold to someone at City Island. In another family, the father was going to college at night." The teacher, she feels, is very much respected. "Usually when I visit, only the father speaks to me; the wife and children sit back quietly. The girls in class, too, sit back while the boys do most of the talking.

"I love living in Franklin Plaza. I wanted to live here even before I found out how fascinating the neighborhood is. The people are sweet and they really care. They come out to organizational meetings and really work. If the women didn't have to worry so much about family matters—having boy friends, or problems with their husbands—they could do much more. They feel freer when they come to New York. They make more money and have better things, and they get wilder. The next generation will be much more settled."

Her only complaint about East Harlem is that it could be "visually more attractive."

Another young white woman resident of Franklin Plaza and an active member of the cooperative describes her thoughts and feelings, which seem to be typical:

The cooperation that's needed is for everybody to be willing to live in these buildings, not just white people, not just Chinese, but everybody. Integrate all races into the building. This way the people are going to get to know each other.

The only danger we really have heard is like the teen-agers over there that start trouble. That's natural. Boys do start trouble with each other. I've lived in three or four different neighborhoods. And there has been violence in each one. I've lived in Yorkville, and it's supposed to be pretty exclusive, and they were robbing every night. I lived in Long Island, and there was a gang killing right around the corner from my house. Here I can walk from *my* house to *her* house any hour of the day or night and not be afraid to walk out.

The community is improving all the time, as people learn that we're not here to lord it over them because we're middle income. We're getting to the point where—we live here and you live there— and it's a mutual cooperation type of thing. Antagonism is lessening all the time.

A PERSPECTIVE ON ACTION AND INITIATIVE

Does it work? Do these various help, self-help, and protest projects produce results? Which of them produce the best results?

All we have now are guesses and observations. There is no final proof. Community action in the city is still in a "demonstration" phase. No means of sound scientific evaluation has been built into any of the projects. Aside from a few crude indexes (number of voters, income, employment, condition of schools, housing, crime and delinquency rates), it is doubtful that such means exist.

In judging these efforts, what matters is the number of people who rise above poverty, not the number of people who go to meetings or join organizations. The meetings are simply a means to an end. It may be assumed that the more frequently and intensely citizens participate in the affairs of their community, the more likely they will be to get what they want. People in motion may move off in the wrong direction, however—or they may run for one day and lie down for six or forever, out of sheer fatigue. The intensity or volume of activity, therefore, is not always a good predictor of successful results.

Only one certain judgment can be made. None of the projects in motion now strikes directly at the heart of poverty—jobs, abundant jobs at decent wages. But poverty has many sub-problems, and it is at these targets that current projects are aimed. Any final evaluation of urban action programs is premature and unfair to their advocates. The lower east side's Mobilization for Youth project was almost analyzed into the grave before it was born. Even with time, evaluation is difficult. The Industrial Area Foundation's work (see Chapter 8), for example, cannot always be judged by the end product. Back of the Yards, once considered I.A.F.'s biggest success, has become a rigidly exclusionist and racist community. Nor did the Chelsea project, the I.A.F.'s only New York effort, turn out well. Even TWO did not beat renewal as it set out to do, but it did gain ground and it did mobilize the community. Now the question is: How much will this arousal help the community to emerge from poverty?

Protest has helped break down the wall of invisibility that separates the poor from the outside world. It has called public attention to their problems, and it has helped organize the poor. As the nation turns its attention to the slum, the street protest and the loud noise will become less necessary. If Negroes can get decent jobs and some real power and voice in decision-making, they will have less urge and need to demonstrate.

A mass-based democratic community organization—I.A.F. style or not—is obviously an asset in any impoverished community. It gives the community strength and a loud voice. In some communities, political organizations come close to offering this.

As for Preston Wilcox and the East Harlem Project: Organizing people without agitation is slow and difficult. People have been put in touch with each other, especially in public housing, and they have become better neighbors and better tenants as a result. They have also learned how to get some of the things they want from their "landlord." Other groups, organized by the Project, have learned how to get some things from the schools; and, in the process, they have learned how to work together for community uplift. All have helped reduce the appalling anonymity of New York apartment living—an anonymity that ignores crime and generates loneliness, hostility, and emotional distress.

The Project has not produced a mass, communitywide organization, and it does not seem headed in that direction. It has not obtained massive outside aid yet (as Haryou did), nor has it successfully organized in tenements where the worst poverty is found. In bringing people together, however, it has helped plant the seed for such organization.

Using protest and agitation, one man, working alone, can do much to organize a community—as I.A.F. organizers do. Without these means of stirring up people, and getting them to stir up others, much more help is needed. The public can easily afford to give that help. If, for example, the federal government can support university rural extension programs that assign five hundred men to rural Michigan alone, it can afford to send comparable numbers into communities such as East Harlem.

As for the community school, I believe that the school—as the most valued community resource and one of the few that exists in many slums—can make large contributions to the community's development. In order to do this, the school staff must expect, hope for, and welcome not only participation from the community, but criticism and protest. If it comes, they will know they are successful. If it does not, then people in the community simply don't care, don't trust the school, and won't talk. If people in slum communities seem happy with slum schools and content with their children's progress, then something is wrong. Probably what is wrong is that citizens have no channel through which they can express opinions and grievances.

Parents, of course, will blame the school for some things that are not the school's fault but, if the school wants to reach parents and affect the "home conditions" of children which they say is retarding their learning, then they will have to encourage and listen to these protests, without feeling under personal attack.

The community school can reach parents and make them friends, allies, and participants. It can encourage them to carry on other community projects. It can provide a meeting place, a forum, a recreation and adult education center. In many schools, however, the impetus for parent and citizen organization around school issues will have to come from outside the schools. The schools will open after hours for recreation and education, but they may not encourage or permit parents to take part in educational decision-making.*

What seems most productive in all these projects is the development of indigenous leadership. By far the best example of this I have seen was sponsored neither by public nor private agencies but by the Negro leadership within Detroit's labor movement. The Trade Union Leadership Council contains all the elements of other projects, and it originates in indigenous leadership. It is a mass citywide organization. It uses protest sparingly and then only to achieve certain ends, not for its own sake. It is essentially a political organization and wields real political power.

Any organization that is successful among the poor must, finally, be political in direction and tied in with a national political movement. The "results" the poor seek can come only with government action—federal action in particular—to provide economic planning for full employment, improved economic growth rates, vastly improved educational opportunities, and decent social legislation.

* It is significant that the most commonly encountered grievance of parents has to do with the physical abuse and punishment of children. This is also the most serious grievance against police. If parents were called upon to help "keep order" in the school and in the neighborhood, the sources of disorder and of both grievances would probably diminish.

10

Politics and Policy

The federal poverty program, like the civil rights bill, was a political response to the accumulating protest and electoral power of Negroes and other poor. The program is not likely to make a notable dent in East Harlem's poverty. Funds are too limited. Federal demonstration programs can show, however, that the poor need not always be among us and that there is a way out, given sufficient desire and funds.

East Harlem alone can probably turn up half of the 40,000 youths recruited nationally for the Job Corps program, but there are only a few hundred openings for East Harlem youth. Thousands of unskilled jobs must be created in that community alone to meet the work need.

Langston Hughes suggested that the young men of Central Harlem be put to work cleaning up their streets, backyards, alleys. East Harlem could use such a project also and could employ youths in such jobs under the work-training provisions of the federal poverty law. But again, while East Harlem can supply ten or twenty thousand applicants for such work, it gets no more than a few hundred jobs.

The work-study provisions of the bill, designed to help youths from poor families go to college, do not have much effect in East Harlem since so few of its residents ever get that far in school. But if the community and city colleges would focus on this provision of the federal program as a way to get under-privileged youths to apply and qualify for admission, it could stimulate at least a few hundred of East Harlem's young people to go to college.

Job agencies are deluged with applicants, especially young ones, so it is apparent that the poor want to work. Most agencies offer counseling, testing, referral; few create new jobs except for job counselors. New York City has had about 300,000 un-employed—some 77,000 between the ages of 16 and 21, most of them school dropouts. Many more would enter the job market if there were jobs. More than half a million jobs must be created in New York City alone.*

In New York the state commissioner of education has pre-dicted that in seven years 1 million youths in the state will be competing for 200,000 unskilled and semiskilled jobs.

The doubters say that our economy cannot produce many more unskilled jobs, except for busy work, and that the press of the job market is for more skilled and white collar jobs and fewer unskilled manual jobs. Even so, unmet needs for unskilled workers are visible everywhere. The slums and the cities need to be cleaned and fixed up. Filling unmet school and housing needs could provide hundreds of thousands of semiskilled jobs.

* Training programs are now simply scratching the surface of unemploy-ment. In one recent year, local offices of state employment services screened 107,500 for training under the Manpower Act. Of these, 22,700 were tenta-tively identified for referral after screening; 8,955 were actually referred for training, of which 6,315 actually enrolled in courses. There were 3,700,000 unemployed at the time.

It has been suggested that returning to two or three postal deliveries a day would create thousands of unskilled jobs and speed the flow of business. The needs are there; public planning is wanted to convert them into jobs for the impoverished.

The federal volunteer program can be used to organize and supervise summer and after-school activities and thus help many improve their school performance, but again the numbers involved are not large enough to have a significant effect on education.

The poverty program is a demonstration project, and it is worth doing, even on a limited scale. Perhaps if it is well done, Congress may be encouraged to believe that money appropriated to help take the poor off welfare and raise them out of the slums is, in the long run, money invested rather than spent.

JOBS

What profit hath a man of all his labors
which he taketh under the sun?
—ECCLESIASTES

The political response has not yet attacked the source of poverty—jobs. Protest has skirted the job issue except for pressure on the skilled trades. In East Harlem almost every issue has been taken on except this one: decent jobs at decent wages, jobs that would enable the poor to afford better housing, education, physical and mental care. The poor have been led to believe that the fault is theirs, that if they would only learn skills they could get decent jobs. In fact, there are not enough skilled jobs for everyone who wants a decent job. There are many skilled jobs available—for which the poor might train—but not enough, not nearly enough. Unskilled jobs are needed, in large quantity, to meet the need. The nation's economy is too sluggish and the public and private sectors too unenterprising to produce unskilled jobs in the quantities needed. An economy which is planned and pushed, as it was during World War II when almost all the poor were employed at decent unskilled jobs, seems to be a national necessity.

Political action has won jobs in government for Negroes and other poor. One out of nine employed Negroes in New York works for the city, compared with one out of twenty whites. Puerto Ricans are underemployed in New York City. While they are 8 per cent of the city's population they hold only 3 per cent of city jobs.* In East Harlem three out of four men are in the labor force, and about one out of ten of these available men are unemployed.

Large and young families handicap East Harlem's poor. They raise expenses while taking a potential wage earner, the woman, out of the labor force. In East Harlem only 35 per cent of women are in the work force. In a nearby middle class community, 57 per cent of women are in the job market. Both the jobs and the women are more available for work. Since a second income in a family can make the difference between poverty and plenty, day care centers for the children of working mothers would enable East Harlem women to supplement family earnings.

Among the most successful job programs has been the employment of indigenous leaders as "subprofessionals" within the community. In relatively brief training programs they are prepared to organize, educate, and perform certain jobs in the

---

* New York City is the second largest employer of Negroes in the nation; only the federal government employs more. A high proportion of Negroes in government are white collar workers. The proportion employed in professional jobs is twice as high in public as in private work in New York City. More than half of all Negroes in New York City's labor force have white collar jobs, mainly in public service.

In a 1964 survey of city departments, Police Commissioner Michael J. Murphy was among those who would not make a racial census. He said the survey smacked of racism. Estimates put the number of Negro police at 1,300 out of a total of 26,171, with about 700 Puerto Ricans. The Transit Authority also refused to take a census, but an estimated 700 Negroes and 200 Puerto Ricans were among its 34,984 employees. The highest proportion of Negroes was found in the Department of Hospitals.

In New York, Negroes held 23 per cent of city jobs; in Philadelphia, 40 per cent; Detroit, 35 per cent; Chicago, 20–25 per cent.

schools and in social work and recreation programs. Because they *are* indigenous to the community they often perform these jobs better than more highly trained outsiders. The idea needs to be applied to other types of community work.

THE SOCIAL WORKER AND THE ORGANIZER

Social workers have been the target of much abuse, both earned and undeserved. Social workers, whose profession is tending the poor and troubled, have not turned poverty into abundance. But nobody expected them or encouraged them to do it. Nor have they brought the poor to public attention. That job was done by such men as writer Michael Harrington and economist Leon Keyserling.

Welfare and social workers have been called "colonialists"— imposing agency charity on a reluctant public and making the poor more dependent. A peripheral truth lurks here, but the central truth is elsewhere. Welfare is not a cure for poverty. Only decent jobs, housing, schools can cure. Even as palliatives the social worker's salves have been much too thin and mis-applied to soothe the wounds of the poor. Much of the resources of social agencies have gone to the less, rather than the more, needy. For example, East Harlem's most desperately im-poverished subarea, the Triangle, is almost barren of social agencies.

The charge against social workers which sticks best is that they seldom go in for either social action or self-help. They rarely organize the poor, consult them, or encourage their initiative. Neglect of protest may be excused by the conserva-tism of recent history, but neglect of self-help for the poor is harder to pass over.

The new militants use the term "social work" as a curse. "It is not surprising," wrote Charles Silberman,* "that the 'child-adults' who inhabit the slums hate the colonial administrators who came to 'uplift' them through 'social discipline,' or that

* *Crisis in Black and White*, New York: Random House, 1964.

they try to sabotage the disciplinarian's program." He reports one East Harlem youth as saying, "They're all around the neighborhood [social workers] and most of them are rat-fink types." This is strong. Some East Harlem residents hate social workers, no doubt, but many more regard them as minor nuisances, do-gooders and outsiders who don't really know the score and don't care. Many are respected and liked, but too often their "image" and the work they do seems on the weaker side of mediocre.

The mobilizers believe that slum revival will come through mass rather than individual action—collective behavior and small-group action rather than individual or family therapy or casework. The usual social work methods, they believe, are as effective in combating mass poverty as a spear is in knocking out armored tanks.

The poor, some claim, often suffer emotional distress because they are estranged from the people closest to them. They stand, essentially, as lone and hostile individuals. Mass action, especially in conflict with an "outside enemy," it is further claimed, can draw people together and give them purpose and a sense of group identity; and it can give a new direction to the "apathetic" or hostile person whose anger may be turned in on himself or those near him. "Only when the individual feels he is a worthwhile member of a worthwhile group does the risk of mental illness drop to a low point," said Dr. Alexander H. Leighton after a ten-year study of mental illness. The poor find personal as well as social power in solidarity.

When people get together, the power progression is often geometric. Ten organized individuals may have 100 times the strength of the sum of each detached unit. Adolescent boys show they know this when they form gangs. Workers show they know this when they form unions.

The psychoanalytic approach that dominates social casework, however, sees flaws in the early childhood and parent-child relations of the poor—and offers "understanding" as a solution. The organizers offer social reform and system reform.

The claim that the poor are getting an excess of social service did not match with the experience of East Harlem. It is true that the *New York City Directory of Social and Health Agencies* contain 721 pages. And in Harlem–Upper Manhattan, the Protestant Council of the New York reported, there were 156 separate agencies serving an estimated 240,000 people, or roughly "40 percent of the total population of the area." These grand totals are misleading. The area cited includes many white, middle class sections, and agency reports of the number of people serviced are notoriously inaccurate and overlapping. The same people show up in the counts of many agencies, and the great majority of troubled people in East Harlem appear to receive no agency help at all. It it claimed, for example, that no agency in Upper Manhattan, except the Urban League, is concerned exclusively with the Negro family, despite the general belief that distress in the Negro family causes much difficulty.

Protest—even when it turns its guns on "welfare colonialism" —often comes round to demanding more and better welfare. Some ministers in East Harlem complain about the surplus of social workers and end by asking for more. The poor need more and better service, and they need to take the initiative in demanding services. In this way they may preserve their tattered pride and make welfare more nearly what it should be for the dispossessed—a matter of right, not charity. That welfare has been simply charity is not the fault of the social worker but of the law. Only recently was rehabilitation written into the law; before that is was simply charity.

The protest of East River CORE led to the formation of a welfare complaint and referral clinic. "We'd like to have people in the community who are on welfare be incorporated into this program," a CORE worker said. "Welfare doesn't seem to be staffed adequately, so we can help." CORE wanted welfare workers to move clients out of East Harlem into integrated areas where they could get better housing at lower cost. "Welfare does not take it upon itself to push integration. They just keep moving people around in the ghetto."

"We also found that in many cases welfare workers just

don't care at all," said a CORE youth. "They are overwhelmed and not particularly interested in the community in the first place. You find a lot of hostility on the part of the welfare worker toward the tenant. Sometimes they won't come up. When they do come up, often they don't really try to help their client. He's asked to come all the way up here to work in the ghetto, and maybe he doesn't like working here. Then he puts off everything on his client."

The CORE worker's comments about welfare policy and personnel seem more common than unique. Many complaints about welfare, concerning these and other matters, are heard. However accurate or justified, they are pervasive.

One family of eight was living in two rooms. CORE persuaded the welfare worker to move them to better quarters. "The particular welfare worker was not mean. She just was not very creative or responsive to her client." One CORE captain found a slum building where every tenant was on welfare. When he suggested a rent strike, the worker was ready to cooperate. The rent was withheld by Welfare, and the building was repaired.

"Welfare tries to be the most noncontroversial agency in the city. They don't want to go out of their way to cause any kind of problem." Social workers have sounded no alarm, but they are responding, less drowsily than most professionals, to the call for social action that has come out of the new mass movements. When they can no longer easily be blamed for the woes of the poor, criticism may turn to more substantive matters, to the economy and to a system that produces and tolerates poverty.

BIRTH AND FAMILY

Economists refer to the triple social revolution. A fourth revolution, for the poor at least, may be birth control. Large families and illegitimacies among the poor are often undesired, but birth control and the numerous unwanted children are still almost unmentioned subjects in East Harlem.

New York's Welfare Commissioner James R. Dumpson (a Negro and a Roman Catholic) budged slightly off a policy that strictly denied birth control information to welfare recipients. Such information is now given, but only to women living with their husbands, thereby excluding four out of five relief families. Those seeking information are given a list of hospitals providing it. "Personally, I oppose birth control," Dumpson said.*

Other serious stresses are seen in the family. It has, in fact, undergone such intolerable strains in industrial society that it may not be able to hold up under them, and the religious and social work emphasis on "strengthening the family" may fail to prop it up. Perhaps the family, as we know it, can no longer carry its heavy burden: sustenance, stability, socialization. Voluntary alternatives, such as that offered by the Israeli *kibbutz*, might be useful experimental substitutes.

THE COMMUNITY CONCEPT

In London local councils run their own housing and education. In New York and other U.S. cities, the local communities have almost no control of their own affairs. Decentralization and neighborhood autonomy in the city are favored by some poor areas as a means of organizing and building the community and protecting it against urban renewal. Autonomy is also favored by some white middle class neighborhoods as a means of preserving the *status quo* in their racially and economically segregated neighborhoods.

As Manhattan borough president, Robert Wagner, in 1951, set up twelve community planning boards in Manhattan to advise local officials on community issues. In 1964, Wagner as mayor proposed that a city hall be set up in each neighborhood

---

* In the past two decades, illegitimacy has reportedly increased by 300 per cent. In 1961 about one of five mothers receiving aid-to-dependent-children (ADC) assistance was not married; in 67 per cent of families the father was absent from the home. Distribution of ADC only to fatherless families has given an incentive to desertion and thus falsely inflated the illegitimacy statistics.

of the city, to house all city agencies in one central place and make government more accessible to the people. All local matters would be sent to these boards for discussion and advice thirty days prior to hearings before the city's Board of Estimate or Planning Commission. To improve coordination neighborhood offices of all city departments—police, fire, welfare, education, etc.—would have the same boundaries. Municipal government, it was proposed, should set standards and allocate money, and the local community boards would set up neighborhood programs. Swedish-type complaint boards, others have suggested, should be set up to deal with grievances against government bureaus.

East Harlem's planning board, headed by Bill Kirk of Union Settlement, is among the few appointed in 1951 that are still active. Professionals dominate the board, though a number of local citizens attend meetings. The local boards, some charge, have strengthened the "neighborhood school" and *de facto* segregation. Others claim that local boards have, through responsible public discussion of issues, helped deflect the more extreme segregationist sentiment. Local boards in such places as East Harlem offer a badly needed voice and organization for the community.

Organized communities tend to be exclusionist. The closer people are to each other, it seems, the more resistant is their response to suspicious or undesired outsiders. The Irish and Polish working class community organized by Saul Alinsky in Back of the Yards, for example, became so tightly organized that it is now an oasis of segregation and racial exclusion in central Chicago. Unless contrary forces are brought to bear—religious, educational, moral—the organized community may itself become a walled ghetto.

Lack of integrated organization, however, can be dangerous to a community and can keep it powerless and impoverished. The self-destructive riots in Central Harlem might not have occurred had that community not been splintered into so many feuding parts but had possessed, instead, an organized and integrated core, which was responsible, democratically elected, and influential both in the neighborhood and in the larger community. Such riots are unlikely to occur in a city like Detroit, for example, where the Negro community is now effectively and democratically organized and where it has much political influence in local government.*

East Harlem is poor partly because it is poorly organized for action in its own self-interests. Though professionals have put many people in touch with each other, it has not yet yielded much neighborhood spirit. It is this spirit—joining with others and trusting others— that shields newcomers from the crippling anomie of the big city, the sense of being adrift in a strange and dangerous place, without purpose or ties, with no place to go and no roots to hold you steady.

East Harlem is itself a big city, too big to be a neighborhood, and it too needs to be decentralized. It also needs a more coherent central authority. It is cut up by city departments into a dozen different jigsaw patterns. There is no single seat of local government. East Harlem contains two postal zones, two police precincts, two school districts, two park districts, two welfare districts, two hospital districts, etc. Almost none have congruent boundaries, and the offices of each are scattered. Even the experts can't keep track, let alone the impoverished rural migrant.

Like other inner-city slums, East Harlem has been a staging area in the past. One wave of poor immigrants has given way to the next and moved out and up to better neighborhoods. Now that the Puerto Rican migration has almost ended and the Negro migration slowed down, East Harlem is struggling to become a stable and mixed community, a decent place to live and perhaps even raise children. It wants long-term rather

---

* Ten of New York City's communities are so seriously impacted by social disorganization that only large-scale efforts, it is believed, designed to modify underlying causes can be expected to have any significant results. The areas are: Harlem, East Harlem, Lower East Side, Bedford-Stuyvesant, South Bronx, South Jamaica, Brownsville, Williamsburg, Astoria, Morrisania.

than transient residents. The strategy for East Harlem is to lift it out of poverty by holding on to the upwardly mobile who would otherwise move out, bringing in middle class residents, upgrading the conditions of the poor. The city's intention to help Manhattan climb uphill will also very likely give East Harlem a boost along its way.

THE IMAGE OF POVERTY

Public image seems as much a concern of East Harlem as of Madison Avenue. Speaking for the negative image, Percival Goodman once said at an East Harlem meeting: "This whole area is in a hell of a mess. It's in a hell of a mess socially. It's in a hell of a mess morally. It's in a hell of a mess physically."

Speaking for the affirmative, Herman Badillo, Commissioner of Relocation and for some years the highest placed Puerto Rican official in New York said: "We find that those of us who live and work in East Harlem and who come into daily contact with it, see it quite differently from the 'outsiders'—the people who only ride through on their way to work, or who read about it in their daily papers. These so-called 'outsiders' look upon East Harlem as a blighted, undesirable community destined to remain an eyesore on the skyline of our city. We who live and work here, however, see East Harlem as a vital, exciting community, needing help and improvement, true, but help and improvement which has the overwhelming aim to seek out and identify this vitality and find ways to conserve, improve and expand it."

Central Harlem and Haryou stress the negatives—the potential for violence—and demand public aid. East Harlem stresses the positives, tries to build on strengths, and hopes to woo voluntary participation and develop community spirit. The negative image shakes up the complacent and the positive one encourages the striver. One is the way of protest, the other of self-help. East Harlem's way is more the Puerto Rican way. It remains to be seen which image will more effectively upgrade a community. To date, Central Harlem has made a lot of noise and received a lot of money. East Harlem has made no noise and received no money. Yet in a sense, because East Harlem is poorer and because it is *not* a racially segregated ghetto, it deserves more public support than Central Harlem.

The debate over whether East Harlem should be called a slum (whether it *is* a slum) is part of the effort to upgrade it. Some merchants, social workers, and others want to take the "slum" curse off and give it a better name. They like statements such as this, made by a YMCA worker about Central Harlem: "Let me say that I love Harlem. I live in it and it is one of the richest communities in the city from the standpoint of its culture, its organizations, its agencies and its people. It has problems, but it is rich." They and others criticize the "negativism" of the Haryou report on Central Harlem which uses this language in describing the community: "Immobility, stagnation, apathy, indifference and defeatism are among the more obvious consequences of person and community impotence. Random hostility, aggression, self-hatred, suspiciousness, seething turmoil, and chronic personal and social tensions also result from powerlessness."

The observer is torn: Calling a slum a rose will not make it pink and perfumed, but calling it a slum won't make it smell better either. Some people in East Harlem think a slum is a slum and that a spotlight should be thrown on the rats, roaches, and tenements in order to get rid of them. Under bright lights, however, the vermin may simply scurry for cover and emerge again in the dark.

One of my first encounters in East Harlem was with its public image. Looking for a place to live (not an easy job) I applied to the East Harlem Protestant Parish for help. There I ran headon into suspicion of writers and other publicists who might relay horror stories about the slum, smearing the community and the parish with it.

Despite their fears, these good Christians offered tentatively to rent me one of their apartments. To get the apartment I had to appear before their board, where I was questioned about what I was going to write, what I had written before, what I would say about the community, how I would conduct my research, what I thought of East Harlem, and "why didn't I write about some good people in the parish who had raised themselves up and become good citizens?"

I did not get the apartment, though I lived there for three weeks. Homeless, I nevertheless saw their point They had been burned by the "hell-hole" journalist and did not want to put their hands on the flame again.

Strangers do have a false image of East Harlem. They tend to see only negatives. There are more negatives in East Harlem than in most neighborhoods, but there are also many positives— the children, the variety, the simplicity and directness of life, the natural warmth and generosity of many people, and the struggle that makes life meaningful as well as grim. Though East Harlem's residents are housed in symmetrical boxes, the people are not all standardized and prepackaged. They are diverse, colorful, expressive, and often profoundly individualistic.

Traditional scholarly research on the "culture of the deprived" has offered little hope for possible change in this culture, short of cataclysm. Its stress is almost always on the downbeat and the negative. The following description of the culturally deprived summarizes almost all the major scholarly research findings on the "deprived." It is a rather complete summary of the negative features of that culture. And it illustrates the scholar's preoccupation with negatives and the ascriptions of some negatives to the poor that are unearned.

Simplification of the experience world—this world is narrowed to a very limited range through a lack of experience and lack of education. *Powerlessness*—through the lack of requisite skills, knowledge and experience he is unable to utilize those roles which could obtain for him the goals he seeks. *Deprivation*—he lacks the resources relative to felt needs and levels of aspiration. He feels he has fallen short of his ideals in education, job, home, income, happy marriage. *Insecurity*—the irregular and unpredictable occurrence of deprivation. He is less able than others, because of a lack of resources, to cope with those aleatory elements which arise.*

The findings read almost like a list of charges against the poor:

Participation in voluntary associations is more limited for the L.L. ["lower lower class"] than for the other classes.

Preference for the familiar. The L.L. person is reluctant to meet new people and new situations, to form new relationships and to initiate interaction with strangers. He values and seeks out the familiar, the routine, and the predictable. L.L.s worry about what others think of them. They are uncomfortable in new and strange situations. They are limited in the degree to which they can shift perspectives and adopt new roles.

Anti-intellectuality. L.L.s tend to be suspicious of intellectuals and to value them very little. In a class where masculinity is greatly valued, art and intellectuality would appear to be inconsistent with masculinity.

Authoritarianism. L.L.s agreed most strongly with F-Scale [authoritarian scale] items. Role relations . . . are more likely to be defined in concrete terms of superordinate-subordinate [and the L.L. is likely to have] little tolerance for ambiguity.

Intolerance. A variety of scales finds the L.L. individual scoring consistently high on measures of ethnic and racial intolerance.

Pessimism-insecurity. In the L.L.s view . . . nothing is certain. He feels that he has to live for today and let tomorrow take care of itself. He also appears to view the world in a pessimistic way— the lot of the average man is getting worse; the cards are stacked against me, opportunities for success never come my way, etc. However, many L.L.s do achieve success through steady work habits, self-discipline and frugality; the world view of the lower class man is, thus, not always a realistic evaluation of his life chances.

* "Characteristics of the Lower Blue Collar Class," by Albert Cohen and Harold Hodges, summarized by George Bodine, mimeographed statement. The data were obtained from 2,600 male heads of families living in three counties in the San Francisco area.

It is, rather, a rationalization of failure and frustration, and it is self-fulfilling prophecy, for his belief motivates a style of life that insures the experiences of failure and frustration.

Misanthropy. More than any other stratum, L.L.s are cynical and distrustful. This "people are no damn good" theme was supported by responses to several other items. Success, they felt, was most often accomplished through chance, deceit, friends, influence. Your friends will stand by you, but strangers are not to be trusted and most people are strangers. It is an interesting fact that in contrast to this cynical, distrustful nature . . . the L.L. person can also be pictured as being credulous, in that he readily accepts the written or printed word. . . .

Extrapunitiveness. . . . The suggestion is that L.L.s find it easier to impute the fault for faulty outcomes to something outside the self. Aggression which accumulates in response to repeated frustrations is directed "outward" rather than "inward" toward the self. The typical roles of the L.L.s require that they take not only their cues, but their directives, from others. [This facilitates] assigning blame to others when things go wrong.

Patriarchy. L.L. men feel that men should have the responsibility for making important decisions in the family. L.L. subjects also indicate that women take responsibility for budgeting, bill paying and child care.

Toughness. A "dog-eat-dog" ideology, in a sense "tough-mindedness," characterizes the L.L. Toughness also requires an ability to "take it," and to keep people from "pushing me around." There are several ways of dealing with the authoritarian relationships which characterize the social world of the lower class. One way is compliance, obedience, and surrender of autonomy. The polar alternative to this is toughness, i.e. the refusal to surrender autonomy. This way of behaving invites "trouble."

Neighboring. Lower class people engage very little in social activities, but when they do they interact primarily with relatives and neighbors. They appear to be slow in establishing even superficial relationships, but when they do establish social ties with people other than kin, they tend to establish them with neighbors.

While this portrait is all too recognizable and expertly drawn (except for items such as intolerance and authoritarianism that are more complicated than this), we see only the shadows and few of the lights. The only bright spots in this traditional portrait have to do with family:

> The L.L. is able to adjust to his world by forging a network of relations with people who find themselves in similar circumstances. The benefits which are derived from such a network consist broadly of "help in time of trouble." Such can be found at all class levels. However, the L.L. differ from all other class levels in two important ways. First, there is a greater dependence, nearly an exclusive one, on such relationships in the L.L. class. Second, while there is a reoganization of kinship ties upon marriage in the middle class, and even a pruning away of them, this does not occur in the L.L. stratum.
>
> L.L.s interact more with relatives, both absolutely and relative to their interaction with other categories, than other strata. They also claim more relatives who live nearby. However, lower class people also indicate that family life is more unstable and strife-ridden.

These ties of mutual aid and support, plus the strong desire of the poor to get on in the world, are among the slum's many solid building blocks. Herbert Gans, in his book *The Urban Villager*, has shown how strong and deserving of preservation a presumably "deprived slum culture" can be.*

None of the negative qualities are regarded as conscious villainies. They are natural responses to reality. The poor man is cheated by strangers, loan and credit sharks, glib salesmen, sweatshop employers, slum landlords. He does not have connections in the middle class world that offer jobs and opportunities. His "distrust," etc., is thrust upon him, and his buoyancy and good spirits, in the face of this, are all the more positive and remarkable—as is the concern of this sixth grade Puerto Rican boy, resident of an East Harlem tenement:

> I feel sorry for all the bums. They should have a house for them. A family or something. If they had, I bet they wouldn't have anybody go up to them and kick them. If you have a house for the

* New York, The Free Press of Glencoe, 1962.

bums at least they'll have beds. If they see the bums outside on the floor they should take them to someplace, you know, where all the bums could be together and everything, you know, have a nice bed, and comfortable. Sleeping out there, that's terrible. Then when it rains they catch a cold, and they don't hardly have coats or anything.

Where I used to live they had this park where all the bums used to go and they used to take them at certain hours to this big house. There's a place like that. It's called the Bowery—The Bowery— where they take all the bums. So they should bring a truck and pick up all the bums and take them over there. I hear all you have to pay for rent over there is five cents. And then they will give you old clothes. My mother said that if she was rich that every bum she would see she would buy him clothes, you know, and she would buy a house and let them all live there. But the day that you become rich, I'll be a millionaire.

MONEY AND CREDIT

Money is obviously the means of escape from poverty. All too many people are waiting and ready to take it away from the guileless poor who manage to get a job and some income. While the poor will usually shop for cash bargains, they often fall into the trap of credit and interest payments. Consumer education on products, credit, interest rates, savings, and investment is obviously needed.

A Columbia University study of consumers in public housing projects in East Harlem and the Lower East Side showed that the poor seem to be indigent in everything but credit.* Median family income of the five hundred people interviewed was $3,300, with 15 per cent receiving welfare assistance. Only 17 per cent were natives of the city; 45 per cent were Puerto Ricans; 30 per cent, Negroes; and 25 per cent, whites. Only 17 per cent of the family heads had completed high school, and about half had not continued beyond grade school.

* David Caplovitz, *The Poor Pay More*, New York, Free Press of Glencoe, 1963.

Among these poor, because they were able to buy on credit at scalper's interest rates:

Ninety-five per cent owned at least one television set (5 per cent owned more than one).
More than three out of five owned a phonograph.
More than two in five owned a sewing machine.
More than two in five owned an automatic washing machine.
More than a quarter owned a vacuum cleaner.
One in seven families owned an automobile.

Forty per cent paid more than $300 for their TV set and 13 per cent paid more than $400. About two-thirds of these items were bought on credit, and 80 per cent had bought at least one item on credit.

Hardly any shopped for major durables in downtown department stores or in discount houses. They bought instead at local stores that offered easy credit. About half the families bought at least one item from a door-to-door salesman, and more than a third made repeated purchases. About 20 per cent had continuous relations with these salesmen, whom they thought of almost as friends and who did not push hard about payments or add charges when payments were late.

More than 60 per cent had outstanding credit debts. Only 27 per cent had at least $100 in savings. One in five had experienced legal pressures because of missed payments. A larger group—about 40 per cent—had trouble because the merchants did not live up to their obligations. Some 64 per cent said they did not know where to go when they were cheated by merchants.

If they want to buy, the poor are caught in the credit system. These are the terms on which they get credit, the only terms for many. It means they pay too much in purchase price and interest charges. It means they often get inferior merchandise. It also means a drain on savings and a longer road out of poverty.

VOX POPULI

Since the people of East Harlem seldom speak up, the professionals and minority voices are quick to fill in. Their sentiments are not always those of the people. One survey of Negro views in New York City, though not rigorous in its methodology, suggested some avenues for exploring the will of the poor.*

The survey found that Negroes in the ghetto regard "economic complaints" as their biggest problem (54 per cent put it first). Second place was given to housing (49 per cent), third place to crime and criminals (39 per cent), and fourth to education (32 per cent).

Another surprise was that "Negro behavior and attitudes" came in fifth. Almost 30 per cent of respondents said that Negro apathy, indifference, failure to raise children decently were the "biggest problems Negroes have to worry about."†

If these data mean anything, then it can be assumed that there is a very large group within the Negro community that is dissatisfied with some aspects of Negro behavior and that, if responsibility were given them, they would be in a better position to control the unfavorable manifestations.

As for schools, it is often said that most Negroes really do not care about integrated schools, that they want only "good" schools. In the poll, however, 63 per cent said they would rather have their children (if they had any) go to "an integrated school with white children." Only 24 per cent said they wanted "just a good school"; 4 per cent preferred an all-Negro school; and only 7 per cent didn't care or weren't sure.

On busing, opinion was almost split: Forty-six per cent favored having their children "go out of the neighborhood to school by bus and having some white children come by bus to the schools here as a means of getting racial balance in the schools"; 43 per cent opposed it; and 11 per cent were not sure.

* "Attitude of Negroes on Key Questions," *New York Times*, July 27, 1964.
† Since more than one response was sometimes given, the totals add up to more than 100 per cent.

Asked "What is the biggest problem with the schools here in this neighborhood?" more than a third (36 per cent) said they didn't know, that there were no problems, or gave no answer.

Among those who made a specific criticism, the largest percentage (22 per cent) said that overcrowding and split sessions were the biggest problems. Then opinion was evenly split between blame of teachers and blame of parents for indifference and apathy. More than one out of ten (12 per cent) said simply that Negro schools were not as good as white or integrated ones —and, returning to the fear of crime, 9 per cent answered "vicious, hoodlums, crime."

Asked if "Negroes will be able to get equal rights and better jobs and so on" without violence, only 7 per cent said they would have to use violence. On the question of police brutality, 37 per cent were not sure or gave no answer, 12 per cent said there is "a lot," 31 per cent said, "A little," and 20 per cent said, "None at all."

Almost two out of three said that Negroes don't hate whites but don't like them either. A strong thread of hatred appeared however: Six per cent said that most Negroes hate whites, and another 13 per cent said that some Negroes hate whites.

Some social actionists say that Negroes don't care much about integrated housing; yet 44 per cent of respondents said they would rather live in an integrated neighborhood; 10 per cent preferred an all-Negro neighborhood; while 39 per cent said they didn't care.

Almost 70 per cent felt that the civil rights demonstrations had helped Negro chances for equality, and 29 per cent said they take more pride in being a Negro now than they did five or ten years ago (1 per cent said they take less). The most favored civil rights group was the National Association for the Advancement of Colored People (55 per cent gave it a top rating), then CORE (23 per cent), then the Urban League (14 per cent); Martin Luther King was far and away the favored civil rights leader (73 per cent), then Roy Wilkins (22 per cent), then Adam Clayton Powell (21 per cent). These responses merely suggest the avenues of further enquiry that are open to the social scientist.

THE ELEMENTS OF REFORM

Community mobilizers claim that if the people of a community are organized for action, other things will follow—good housing, schools, jobs—that change must proceed from the bottom up, and that the only significant change that can be made with available resources are changes in human behavior and relations. Though many critical observers, including myself, are much impressed with the Industrial Areas Foundation (I.A.F.) style of mobilization (some claim it is the only feasible means of organizing communities), it is doubtful that government projects can or will use these methods. The trials of Manhattan's Mobilization for Youth project, a very subdued version of I.A.F. projects which, in encouraging citizen protest and doing a few other things, stepped on some sensitive political toes, indicate the limitations. Government is not likely to pay for the mobilization of protest against itself, and inherent in such efforts is the threat that the organized and agitated poor will strike out at public officials.

Projects more likely to succeed with public funds are the "supply" projects. Mitchell Sviridoff's Community Progress program in New Haven, Connecticut, is such a project. Public officials in New Haven, unusually responsive to the poor, assumed that as elected officials they had been mandated by the people to do certain things. Unlike the I.A.F. projects, Community Progress is not "run by the people" directly; the link is through the ballot and through previously expressed demand. The voters elected city officials to do certain things, and they did it. Charles Silberman has called the "gray area" projects (including New Haven) a "grandiose fusion of paternalism and bureaucracy." Other observers, including myself, view the New Haven project as extremely creative, effective, and responsive to public demand—whatever its style of decision-making.

Organizing efforts always depend on personalities and places. In New Haven, Sviridoff (a former Auto Workers Union staff member) and city officials are close to the people. Given different personnel and places, such supply projects might fail to reach the people. But mobilization projects, depending on conditions, also fail to reach people, as did the I.A.F. project in New York's Chelsea section.

Ideally, decisions should be made, so far as possible, directly by the people. The people should be the ones to decide what kind of jobs, housing, and so forth they want. In some community organizations and mobilizations, however, a few professionals or organizers with axes to grind do so much manipulation that the will of the people gets less expression than it does through their elected officials. Decisions made by "demand" organizations can be just as controlled, manipulated, and "paternalistic" as those made unilaterally by "supply" organizations. But ideally the people should decide and should not have programs handed down. Some critics charge that in I.A.F. organizations, decisions tend to be controlled by I.A.F. organizers or by the clergy, businessmen, and others who sponsor the projects, and that the people are there mainly to help make a lot of noise. The people, they say, can be just as manipulated by mobilizers as by elected city officials. This is a harsh view, but it has some point. Manipulation is a risk in all organizations.

The role of democratic leadership in community organization needs clear definitions. In the I.A.F., strong agitational leadership is taken by the paid organizer; he has his own issues to sell (often opposition to urban renewal); and he is ready to buy the local issues; his end product is supposed to be a democratic and self-sufficient organization. In the "supply" projects, public officials are elected; and they do all the planning, with only informal checks made with the people. In the East Harlem Project and Puerto Rico's Community Education program, the leader slips off into the background. He gets people together, tells them a few things, but spends almost all his time listening to the people discuss issues and then helping them do the things they say they want to do. Possible flaws in the method are that it is very slow and that it "abdicates leadership" to people who are not in a position to know what the possibilities are and what *can* be done. In one Puerto Rican village I visited, the community had taken four years to decide it wanted a sewage system. This is slow. In most places the poor cannot and should not wait this long for a sewer.

All three approaches have merit and can and should work side by side. Some organizers put more stress on method than on goals. With some, a strange religious mysticism attaches to method. It is not the end for them that counts—the elimination of poverty—but the effect that the method of organization has on human behavior. While the poor need to participate and become autonomous, they need most of all to stop being poor. Any method that will achieve this end will also help make them autonomous. Some of the questions that need answering are: What role should experts play in decision-making? At what stages should *everyone* participate? Is participation for its own sake desirable? How much does broad participation aid in the achievement of personal and community goals?

Though block clubs have been successfully organized among lower income groups in some places, it is not certain under what conditions the New York slum dweller can be organized.* Some people believe that the impoverished tenement dweller is virtually impossible to organize (given present resources) without strong agitation. The poor are apt to be resistant to organization—unless they get fast action and results. Neighborhood Conservation, a city project, has tried to organize tenement

---

* In Detroit almost the entire Negro community is organized into block clubs. That city has a high proportion of home ownership even among families with very modest incomes; the block clubs, organized with help from the city, are mainly concerned about property improvement, though they are now moving into other issues and becoming more political.

tenants for building improvement, but without any notable success. Nor have any other groups in East Harlem had much success in organizing by nonagitational methods. Project tenants have been easier to organize, perhaps because they feel better about themselves and their neighbors and take some hopeful interest in the neighborhood.

On the whole, it seems doubtful that many of the old buildings in East Harlem can be improved much by simply organizing tenants. For those buildings that are worth saving, perhaps cooperative ownership may offer a feasible means of improving conditions.

The poor do not want organization for its own sake, nor should anyone else. They want better housing, better jobs, better schools, etc.—they want results. If organization gets them these things, they will buy it. If government gives them these things, as it should, the poor may not need to organize. Organization is only a means to an end, not an end in itself, though it apparently changes human behavior in a way that few other things can. The simple act of getting people together reduces anonymity and often produces new effort and ideas.

The effectiveness and the effect of organizing need further testing. The techniques of organization also need further exploration. It has been mainly the Marxists who have devoted themselves to the theory and methodology of mass organization —notably Lenin, Trotsky, Kautsky, Luxembourg, Plekhanov, Martov, and others. *Mein Kampf* also dealt with critical questions of organization. These are strategic issues in discussion of social change. In the Russian Social Democratic Party the split between the Bolsheviks and Mensheviks was over such an organizational issue: how the party was to be organized, whether as a revolutionary cadre or a mass organization. These are the issues that, in a real sense, direct and control social change. They deserve much more attention from scholars and men of action.

In East Harlem and other places, CORE is building a community organization among the poor as a balance to its loss of white members and as a means of creating a political organization. It also wants insurance against the probable diminishing effect of the "big issue" demonstration. CORE is working door to door on specific issues that are close to people and around which they can be organized. "The action at the plumbers union [a demonstration over jobs] didn't gain us anything in the community and lost us an awful lot of time. It didn't have anything to do with the people here. And it was downtown, and downtown is another world for most people here." These small issues lead into voter registration and political action, "but it's difficult to convince people that any kind of social action will get them anything except a slap in the face."

The most logical groups to carry on community mobilization and development are the trade unions. This type of organization is a trade union specialty. Instead of organizing on the job they would simply organize in the community.

Unions are autonomous and relatively independent of both public and private establishments. They have staff, experience, and funds for community mobilization. Most important, they have a political program and strong political motivation. The poor need to be "politicalized" and tied into a national political movement. They also have much to gain through connections with organized labor.

The better unions have set up community political groups that resemble community mobilization projects except that they rarely engage in protest or nonelectoral activity; nor do they often concern themsleves with a broad range of community issues.

The organizational formula developed by organized labor has been a prototype for community mobilization. Unions built their powerful organizations and gave a voice and real power to the "then" poor through this simple six-step formula:

1. Listen to the grievances of people; listen to the problems and complaints.

2. Decide what are the best issues to press and organize people around.

3. Use the natural leaders (the men from the shop) to do the organizing, not white collar professionals with a university degree in labor organizing.

4. Arouse the people over these issues—"agitate" them if you will—get them to see that their hope lies in organization.

5. Once organized, engage in mass action which will both unify your own group and exert influence on employers.

6. Press ahead on the political front, where the largest victories are to be won.

With this formula, labor accomplished great feats. It confronted the whole spectrum of industrial and financial power with nonviolent resistance, the strike. It brought decent wages, better working conditions, and more security to the poor who joined its ranks. Some critics may look back and say that such things were not very nice—strikes, disobedience, sometimes violence on the picket line, but few would now deny that organized labor made a valued contribution in bringing democracy into the shop and decent standards to millions of America's impoverished.

Unions are almost absent from the East Harlem scene and do not exist as a community power. Some individual unionists are active, and some community leaders are experienced unionists. The clothing, service, and retail unions to which many East Harlem workers belong are occasionally visible, but only at election time. Some unions donate to a settlement house or buy tickets for charity affairs. Given the nature of unionism, its political direction, experience with protest and self-help organization, views on economic and social issues, organized labor and the poor are natural associates.*

* In 1954, reports Lois Gray of Cornell University, the central federations of labor in the New York area set up a labor advisory committee on Puerto Rican affairs, and from this have grown efforts on the part of many unions to organize Puerto Ricans and encourage their participation. She reports that about 70 Puerto Ricans are working as full-time union officials in New York

Unions and union members contribute vast sums of money to local charity drives and community chests. Through labor sits on the boards of many of these groups, it has not yet insisted that this charity money be used in community organization nor that aid be funneled more into assistance for the genuinely poor and desperate. Many unions have their own community services programs, with national staffs and services to local unions. Even these resources have not been used for the organization of the poor. These groups are in a position to offer leadership. In the Auto Workers union, Andrew Brown, director of community services, has led an effort to organize ADC women in Detroit. The organization will help these women exchange information, keep them from being pushed around and deprived of benefits—and aid them to become independent.*

Unions in the slum community can help in another important way. Unions are masters both of protest and negotiation. While civil rights and other groups have learned much about the protest stage of social action, they are unskilled and inexperienced at negotiations. They do not know how to move in after the street demonstration is over and win what they are after. Nor do they know how best to hook together protest and negotiation. Often the former has no special relationship to the latter, and demonstrations may be carried on and resources depleted without any special thought or hope of being able to negotiate victories or win anything. The demonstration, like the strike, is an ultimate weapon. It is used when other things do not work, and it is used in order to *get* other things to work. It may be that labor now does not use the strike and other techniques of direct action enough and that membership loyalty and participation slip because of this. On the other hand, the protest-

---

City; that in 1948, 51 per cent of adult Puerto Ricans in New York were members of unions; and that one survey showed in 1959 that two out of three Spanish households had one or more members in unions (Lois Gray, "Labor Unions and Puerto Ricans in New York City," September 1963, mimeographed).

* A common characteristic noted in charity recipients is obedience and dependency; ADC mothers often teach their children these qualities.

ers have sometimes overused these ultimate weapons, with an even greater loss, in the end, of membership vitality. People cannot stay in the streets forever. Victories must be won. They must be won through careful planning, strategy, and skillful negotiation. Trade unionists know how to negotiate, and they know how to build permanent organizations out of protest. Their help is needed in the slum.

Unions might succeed at another task where others fail: involving the men—the average male citizens—in community organizations. Social work and related groups reach some women but not many men. The plight of the church is only one case: "Why do we get so few men?" asked a priest at St. Lucy's in his morning sermon. "Jesus was a man. The twelve apostles were men. Nearly all the early Christian martyrs were men. But today . . . ? Today, women come to church, and nice little girls with nice white veils. But men? Where are they?"

Significant upgrading can be done in East Harlem through direct government action, and without further mobilization of demand. Middle class and integrated elements can be introduced directly into the community's bloodstream, as they have been in the middle income cooperative, Franklin Plaza. Government buildings, a community college, cultural centers, meeting places, perhaps a large post office complex—could also be introduced as middle class ballast. Attractive housing, with special rates for teachers, would attract educated community leaders.

The old- and the new-law tenements could be replaced by decent housing that will accommodate both low and middle income families—all in consultation with the community.

As for the many buildings that could be salvaged (brownstones and others)—property could be bought from slumlords by tenants organized for cooperative ownership.

New action proposals have been drawn up in East Harlem. One community development project would set up a citywide Puerto Rican Council for Economic and Social Development to act as a clearing house for a variety of Puerto Rican self-help programs in neighborhoods. The council would define needs and offer technical and professional assistance in working out programs.*

Another proposal for a block community development program in East Harlem wants to help "members of a community learn confidence through solving their own problems and building leadership from their numbers." The greatest problem East Harlem faces, the proposal says, is the "lack of control over, or influence on the vast private system that exploits them and the vast public system that purports to serve them." The assumption is that "outside aid alone cannot change measurably the discouragement at the root of East Harlem's problems. By and large, the present system of aid is a deterrent to the formation of grass roots leadership and direction."

The block development program would "look for ways by which the gap between man and neighbor can be made less awesome. We will seek concerned people and bring them together. We will encourage unconcerned by-standers to become concerned."

The block workers, to be selected from among Peace Corpsmen, community leaders, and youths, would each concentrate on one block. The worker would bring neighbors together who are faced with common problems—tenants of one building, people who shop at one store or whose kids are in trouble. He would search for leaders. He would refer people to social agencies and other sources for aid with their problems. He would make new programs available to the block—nurseries, narcotics stations, health clinics, etc. To reduce control by professionals, the board of directors would be composed only of residents of East Harlem and those who have a nonprofessional interest in the block program; agencies and churches would be represented by lay members. Provision would be made for volunteers.†

---

* "A Proposal for a Self-help Puerto Rican Community Development Project in the City of New York," Puerto Rican Forum, Inc., 296 Fifth Avenue, New York, mimeographed.

† David Borden, "East Harlem Block Community Development Program, first edition, East Harlem Project," mimeographed.

11

The greatest of evils and the worst of crimes is poverty.
—GEORGE BERNARD SHAW

A Final Perspective

I went to East Harlem in ignorance and hope. I came away less ignorant and no less hopeful. I saw things that most Americans miss. I saw what the poverty of the slum can mean in suffering and squalor, and I saw what it can mean in human warmth, life, diversity, color.

Many things are needed in East Harlem. One of them is volunteers. It is tragic that so few New Yorkers take a hand, as volunteer residents and workers, in helping people achieve their own end—the remaking of East Harlem. Despite the resistance of some community leaders to "outsiders"—despite professionals who fear invasion of their territory and organizers who think nobody can do anything but them—a big volunteer program is needed in East Harlem. Such volunteers would aid in the community's uplift and in the exchange of views between the haves and have-nots. Methods and means of communication must be found so that the middle class—volunteers, teachers, social workers, etc.—can work and live in close rapport with the poor.

Everyone can fight in this war against poverty. Only the will and the weapons are needed. The arsenals contain a variety of weapons. Each will have its special use, and all will be needed: protest, self-help, charity, organization, volunteers, agency programs, legal action, intelligent renewal, public and private aid. The strategic weapon, however—the nuclear arsenal—will be federal economic policy. Federal poverty programs and decent social legislation are only minor strategic weapons. The major one is economic policy: planned growth, creation of needed jobs —both skilled and unskilled—and redistribution of wealth so that the poor may get their just share of the nation's resources.

Developing this weapon will take a lot of work. It will, above all, require political action on the part of the poor. The community action programs—organizing, developing, mobilizing— will, hopefully, lead into this political action. With political power, the nation's six major and interrelated problems can be taken hold of: economic planning for full employment, the squalor of urban communities, education, civil rights, poverty, reapportionment.

Work done with the residents of slum communities should aim at two targets: giving the poor a sense that they can, through their own initiative (and political action), affect the world around them, and giving the poor a sense that they can, through solidarity with others, organize to alter successfully their environment. Individual initiative, group initiative, and political action: These are also major weapons. The beginning of salvation for the poor will be the realization that they can, through their own initiative and effort—and not by depending on hand-me-downs from higher authorities—control their own destinies. Just as this sense of power is essential to health and happiness, so is it essential to prosperity. Renewal and other outside aid programs must keep this in mind. They must give the poor materials and a physical environment that they can shape and change. Such an environment will not resemble the endless blocks of symmetrical and identical brick towers that are now found in East Harlem (and—even more so—in Moscow and other Russian cities where the city planners have taken over); it will look like a community where the people who have to live in a building have had some say about the building's plan, and a chance to put their own personal mark on it.

In every city of the nation, communities such as East Harlem have been untouched by the tidal wave of national prosperity. The people living in these areas are burdened but not defeated. Given a chance they can do as well, or better, than the rest of us.

Appendix I

A Private Survey of
Housing Violations

The Women's City Club looked into code enforcement in five new-law tenements. Median monthly rent in the 140 apartments of these five buildings was $36, with a range from $21 to $69.

The women interviewed tenants in 59 apartments door to door. They concluded: "The tenants themselves were charming, friendly people who were ashamed of the condition of their apartment, and who maintained that they had no grievance against the landlord."

They found in these 59 apartments, which had been "cleared" by building inspectors less than a year and a half before: 1,319 violations of the housing codes, over half the apartments in fairly poor to very poor condition, 347 hazardous or potentially hazardous violations, every apartment with at least one such violation.

Half of the violations reported by city inspectors were reported again by the women's club.*

* *Maintaining Decent Dwellings. A Study of Code Enforcement in Five New-Law Tenements,* Women's City Club of New York, Inc., 6 West 48 Street, April 1963.

Over two hundred attempts were made to gain access to the apartments. "An 'attempt' involved feeling one's way to the rear of a dark or dimly lit hallway on the ground floor, or climbing one to five flights of stairs to an upper floor (where the light was better) and knocking at the door." Door bells were usually absent or out of order.

The worst apartment showed the following violations: Living room and bathroom walls were broken, the surfaces loose, shaky, and dirty. Paint was missing and peeling and not uniform in color. The kitchen floor was loose and shaky, and the surfaces of floors were broken or cracked.

Window frames in all three rooms were rotten. Some were broken and shaky. One window was inoperable. The kitchen had surface and dangling wires. The bathroom had a cracked, unsanitary bowl, with a leak in the flushing apparatus, a nonfunctioning light and a door that did not close properly. The apartment entrance door was not self-closing or sturdy and had no adequate lock or latch.

"Add to this the presence of rats and vermin, and it is difficult, to say the least, to find any evidence of the enforcement of a housing code."

There were thirty-three cases of rat infestation in the fifty-nine apartments.

In New York all of the city departments (Health, Buildings, Water, Fire, etc.) made *separate* building inspections. Their reports often overlapped and conflicted. "Less than two weeks after a long list of hazardous violations was reported by one department, the fire inspector reported just one violation in all five buildings." Tenants had to know which of half a dozen departments to call. Inspections were made *only* on request of complaining tenants.

The women were "solemnly warned by the City inspectors that they were, under no circumstances, to inspect cellars and roofs. These areas, frequent meeting and hiding places for addicts and criminals, are considered so unsafe, that the inspectors themselves cannot visit them without considerable risk."*

---

* The club has also issued a guide to the bewildering array of housing agencies in the city: *Housing Primer*, Women's City Club of New York, Inc., February 1964.

Appendix II

Failure to Vote

In several cities with large minority populations voting in the 1960 election was:

Congres- sional District	Per Cent Voting Age Registered	Per Cent of Registered Voters Not Voting	Per Cent of Democratic Vote as Per Cent of Total Vote	Per Cent of Voting Age Population That Is Nonwhite
New York City (Man- hattan):*				
16	48.4	56.8	77.1	77.2
17	68.0	39.4	48.8	2.1
18	52.9	53.6	63.2	14.4
19	53.4	52.9	69.8	10.0
20	53.0	53.3	67.6	7.7

* In New York, the Sixteenth includes Central Harlem; the Seventeenth is the silk-stocking district; the Eighteenth covers Central Harlem; the Nineteenth, the Lower East and West Side; and the Twentieth, the Upper West Side.

Congressional District	Per Cent Voting Age Registered	Per Cent of Registered Voters Not Voting	Per Cent of Democratic Vote as Per Cent of Total Vote	Per Cent of Voting Age Population That Is Nonwhite
Detroit:				
1	93.4	30.3	86.3	43.3
13	70.6	38.4	72.9	48.1
14	93.9	25.7	61.5	14.7
15	91.2	31.8	76.8	47.6
16	89.3	27.7	63.6	8.1
17	92.8	22.0	53.1	0.6
Philadelphia:				
1	77.1	31.0	76.5	23.9
2	75.3	32.9	71.5	32.6
3	74.7	34.5	69.4	21.7
4	68.1	42.8	78.6	72.5
5	83.1	22.5	61.7	1.7
6	82.8	23.6	60.6	9.3
Chicago:				
1	87.0	29.6	77.4	86.9
2	87.2	32.2	66.7	45.5
3	98.9	22.7	60.1	28.8
4	—	22.7	49.1	6.3
5	97.8	23.8	68.5	5.3
6	94.1	26.6	70.4	33.3
7	85.6	35.5	79.5	36.6
8	87.8	31.3	64.0	0.7
9	83.4	34.9	54.2	9.2
10	—	20.5	44.3	1.4
11	—	20.2	49.8	0.3
12	94.2	26.6	55.8	1.5
13	—	19.9	37.8	2.8
14	—	23.5	32.6	1.1

Appendix III

Sources of Bibliographies on Community Development and Organization

Community Development Bibiography, Daniel J. Schler, University of Missouri, Columbia, Missouri

Community Development—Rural and Urban, A Selective Bibliography, compiled for the Eleventh International Conference of Social Work by Arthur Dunham, Professor of Community Organization, School of Social Work, the University of Michigan, Ann Arbor, Michigan. Issued by the International Conference of Social Work, 345 East 46 Street, New York, N. Y. 10017, May 1961.

United Nations Series on Community Development, Selective Book List, UN, New York, 1960, ST/SOA/ SER. 0/33

Bibliography in Richard Waverly Poston, *Democracy Speaks Many Tongues,* Harper & Row, 1962.

Information on Puerto Rican education projects can be obtained from Department of Education, Division of Community Education, P.O. Box 432, San Juan, Puerto Rico.

Sample mimeographed questionnaires for obtaining information about neighborhoods can be obtained from United Neighborhood Houses, 114 East 32 Street, New York, N.Y. 10016.

Index